Stonework: maintenance and surface repair

Stonework: maintenance and surface repair

A.D.R. Caroe and M.B. Caroe

2nd edition

CHURCH HOUSE
PUBLISHING

Church House Publishing
Church House
Great Smith Street
London
SW1P 3NZ

ISBN 0 7151 7582 3

Published 1984 for the Council for
the Care of Churches of the
Church of England by Church
House Publishing.

Second edition published 2001.

Designed by Visible Edge, London
Typeset in 9.5 pt Sabon
Printed by Halstan & Co. Ltd,
Amersham, Bucks

Contents

List of Illustrations

Acknowledgements

Amongst the many persons who have helped to produce this summary, the authors would particularly like to thank Mr John Ashurst, Mr David Honeyborne and Dr Clifford Price.

Preface
to the second edition

The text of this publication was prepared shortly after Alban Caroe had retired from his post as architect to the Dean and Chapter of Wells. For the last five years of his professional career, he had been involved almost exclusively on the west front of Wells Cathedral, working in the closest relationship with Professor Robert Baker. Caroe was by then 70 years old and so had a wealth of experience to draw upon; his respect for traditional ways had already been evident in *Old Churches and Modern Craftsmanship*, Oxford University Press, 1948. Since the retirement of Alban Caroe and Robert Baker and the completion of the west front, there has been a massive increase in the availability of finance, research and skills. Whereas in the late 1940s the concept of cleaning a cathedral was generally 'laughable', by the end of the 1990s the development of hydraulic hoists, a greater caution over health and safety, the improvement of surveying and cleaning techniques, and the reassessment of the balance to be struck between conservation and renewal have made certain of the judgements in this booklet appear over-cautious. However, there is so much sound practical sense contained in the original text that we have decided to republish it with only minor changes, but with an appendix of notes that charts development since 1984. While the professionals involved in the maintenance and repair of stonework will have access to the latest technical information, we consider it important to assist the client, whether incumbent, churchwarden, fabric officer or archdeacon, to understand the essential principles that underlie such work.

chapter 1

Introduction

Many of the most significant buildings in England and Wales are churches, both small and large, and the most telling parts of these buildings are often their stone walls and towers. Our appreciation of such stonework often depends largely upon its weathered texture, the product of old craftsmanship mellowed by exposure to the weather: the problems of preserving harmonious weathering while arresting harmful decay become harder with each generation as less and less of the original surface remains intact, while the proportion of later modifications tends to grow steadily larger. Most stone decay is cumulative, and it is obviously harder to maintain continuity in the appearance of an old building when decay is widespread and acute than when it is local and slight. These notes are intended to help architects and others to maintain in good condition the beauties we have inherited and to hand them on to future generations with as little change as possible. One of the best compliments that can be paid to an architect at the end of a successful restoration is when a parishioner wonders how so much money can possibly have been spent with so little apparent effect.

This guide deals only with the maintenance and repair of stone wall surfaces, which means mainly external surfaces since serious superficial stone decay is so much less frequent indoors. The structural repair of walls, considered as a whole and including their cores and their damp-proof courses, will be better covered separately in another publication.

The problems to be faced have altered considerably since the Second World War, and it is worth listing some of the main changes.

- A wide gap has opened up in the building industry between modern standardization and traditional labour-intensive repair. Most of those who still understand old stonework are now considered to be specialists.
- There are fewer skilled masonry firms and masons available in Britain, and labour is not normally prepared to travel so far.

1

In consequence, geographical location can create major difficulties, which hamper the organization of good work in some areas.

- Large sections of the English quarry industry have virtually collapsed, and matching stones are now often unobtainable (though when there are French alternatives they are readily available).[1]
- Aggravated by such factors, the rise in the cost of masonry has been even higher than that due to general inflation.
- Machine tools are being increasingly introduced into the processes of shaping stones and cutting mouldings, in the effort to keep costs down and maintain the viability of the trade. How to benefit from such tools without losing the best qualities of hand craftsmanship raises many problems, but they can be solved.
- There has been a striking decrease in the amount of dirt deposited from the atmosphere; on the other hand harmful acidic sulphur-based pollution has, if anything, increased.[2]
- More synthetic materials are available.
- More skilled advice is available, based on greater scientific understanding of masonry problems.
- More sources of financial assistance are available for masonry repair, but there are also more controls, more form filling, in short, more red tape.[3]

chapter 2
Routine maintenance

Stone decay is relentless, but usually so slow that it is hard to realize when 'the stitch in time' would 'save nine'. Yet many expensive dilapidation repairs would be postponed, or even avoided, if all those responsible for churches not only realized how important routine maintenance is but also acted wisely on their knowledge.

Among the most common routine needs are:
- to stop local saturations of stonework, such as are caused by broken or displaced spouts, eaves gutters, pipes, or blocked parapet gutters;
- to clear blocked ground gutters and drains;
- to prevent rank vegetation (particularly ivy, elder and valerian) growing on the building, and to remove branches of shrubs that touch it;
- to stop rust spreading over iron and steel.

In all these directions much useful work can be done on a do-it-yourself basis, perhaps with some assistance from a local builder. Nevertheless, churchwardens should also remember another adage, 'a little knowledge is a dangerous thing'; for cases occur only too frequently when both extra expense and grave permanent damage are caused to important buildings by minor repairs carried out in good faith but with insufficient knowledge.

Three of the commonest mistakes are:
- repointing stone joints with unsuitable materials and methods. Not only can the result be aesthetically deplorable; even more important is the fact that the use of too hard mortars can greatly accelerate the decay of soft stones;
- allowing any silicone preparation to be applied to stonework in the hope of checking external decay;[1]
- painting on top of rust on iron in contact with stone, a useless precaution and a waste of money.

In all cases of doubt but especially in regard to repointing it will be wise to consult the architect beforehand, at least in principle, even in cases where full supervision by the architect would not be justified.

Moreover it cannot be emphasized too strongly that parochial officials in the Church of England are legally bound to obtain either a Faculty or an Archdeacon's Certificate for most works affecting the fabric of their parish church, and that this obligation covers not only major alterations but also many items of maintenance. Those in doubt should consult either the Archdeacon or the Secretary of the Diocesan Advisory Committee.[2]

chapter 3
Access for repairs

So many factors have tended to raise the cost of good quality stone repair and to reduce the local funds available to pay for it that extensive programmes of stone repair can often be carried out only by phasing them through several decades. Such a gradual approach has moreover other advantages; successive bouts of piecemeal repair involve less sudden changes in the appearance of a building than does one wholesale treatment. On the other hand, it can prove very wasteful not to repair decaying stones when they are easily accessible. Careful planning is necessary to achieve a sound balance between these conflicting factors, and at every stage during the programming and execution of stone repairs the experienced architect remains conscious of the need to consider phasing the works he has in mind. The high cost of scaffolding often becomes a crucial factor in the search for an economical long-term programme.[1]

This is true right from the stage when precise recommendations are being prepared and target estimates are being worked out. Binoculars and ladders have only limited value in helping to decide the extent of stone repair needed more than 20 feet above normal reach, and closer inspection will usually reveal unexpected needs and hazards that will swell the final cost and may cause difficulties if they have not been covered by the accepted tender. It is the architect's constant duty to decide whether time and money will be saved in the long run by additional preliminary expenditure on access for decision making. Cradles or moveable gantries can sometimes help, and in some high-level programmes the erection of light temporary inspection scaffolds can be justified. In the case of spires there is often need to assess the differing merits of employing ordinary masons who will only work off full scaffolds or, alternatively, steeplejacks. In the latter case it is rarely possible to arrange for full supervision.[2]

Maximum economy in the provision of high level access can be even more important during the progress of the contract. Should the scaffold be hired, or bought and resold? How much of the area in question should be scaffolded at any one time, and how long will it pay to keep the scaffold up? What precautions are needed to guard against subsidence of scaffolds carrying heavy weights over damp soil? The architect will ask the scaffolding contractor to ensure that his scaffold meets all requirements under the Health and Safety at Work Act in respect of both workmen and persons below, and also to safeguard the building itself against damage, including such items as rust stains. All reasonable precautions must be taken against theft of lead by vandals utilizing the scaffold to gain access. The extra cost of a materials hoist will be found to pay handsomely in more contracts than might be expected.

chapter 4

Cleaning stonework[1]

Greatly increased importance has been attached during the last 30 years to the value of cleaning dirty and decaying stonework. This has been partly owing to aesthetic reasons, but partly also to civic and personal pride; for many have realized how greatly the appearance of whole districts has been improved by the cleaning of individual buildings within them, and it is no longer considered laughable (as it was in 1948) to consider the possibility of cleaning the whole of a medieval cathedral. In many cases when partial repair or repointing is needed it is impossible to obtain a satisfactory appearance unless whole areas are cleaned, and the extent of such areas needs careful consideration in each case. Cleaning not only makes it possible to appreciate original detail that has been obscured for generations, but also helps the architect to identify defects that may not even have been suspected. It removes some at least of the harmful atmospheric deposits that accelerate stone decay and makes it easier to find replacement materials that will harmonize with the original. When additions or substantial alterations have to be made to an old church, the cleaning of all adjoining surfaces will help to retain the aesthetic unity of the altered building.

But cleaning stonework is far from being a panacea. One should never forget that all stone cleaning involves some risks and it should only be attempted if really necessary for the health of the stone and the appearance of the building. Historic stonework must not be damaged merely in order to obtain a short-term improvement in appearance. Serious harm has been caused by the use of unsuitable or overhurried processes and the acceptance of a cheap tender based upon an inadequate specification can lead too easily to permanent damage. There are many methods of cleaning stonework and the greatest importance should be attached to the selection of the method most appropriate not only to each building but also to each part of each building. Architects may judge it right to ask several firms to submit detailed proposals and tenders and they can draw useful help in assessing the often widely varying technicalities of such proposals from the British Standard Code of Practice for

Cleaning and Surface Repair of Masonry (BS 6270 Part 1, 1982). In cases of real doubt the architect may order trial cleanings of sample areas. In many cases it is wise to vary the methods used or to combine two or more of them as the work proceeds from part to part. Most cleaning contractors are prepared to operate in several ways; alternatively, the general or masonry contractor may be able to carry out some of the cleaning satisfactorily, reserving only the most delicate areas for specialist attention. Masonry firms should be encouraged to undertake as much cleaning as possible, for there are many advantages in such double use of the same labour.

The principal stone cleaning methods now in use are as follows:

Low-pressure water spray

Pure water applied through sprays has for many years been used for cleaning limestones, but it is almost useless on most sandstones and we have become increasingly conscious that there are risks in its use that must be avoided. Over-saturation of stonework can create outbreaks of dry rot in nearby timber, a risk that is particularly great when external walls are thin or contain buried bond-timbers. Even small quantities of water can cause the complete disintegration of delicate stone features whose soft cores are held together only by their sulphated crusts. Water should never be used on stones that have been impregnated with sodium chloride (common salt) nor on any stone when there is risk of serious frost. Pale-coloured limestones such as Portland tend to develop unsightly brown stains about a year after cleaning, but such stains eventually fade. When used with due precautions, clean water sprayed on at low pressure will be found in many cases to be the cheapest way to clean robust limestones with non-specialist labour. Always start at the top and work downwards, taking all feasible steps to reduce the amount of run-off that flows over surfaces below and to ensure its ultimate safe disposal (a particularly important factor when cleaning internally). The quantity of water used should be kept to the minimum found to be effective, and temporary gutters, spouts and other protections should be provided as and where required. The more delicate the stone the more stringent should be the precautions taken against over-saturation, the sprays being softened into mist and applied not continuously but periodically, sometimes only in short bursts. Adjustable timing devices can, in the hands of experts, be useful gadgets to control these bursts. The positions of the spray nozzles need to be changed frequently so as to penetrate into sheltered corners. After the dirt has been thoroughly softened, light brushing (which avoids all scratch marks) will bring dirt off easily on some stones, but others may prove so intractable that other methods of cleaning become essential.

High-pressure water

When there is need to clean limestone ashlar in such durable condition that there is no risk of disintegration, water applied under high pressure (say at 2000 lbs per sq. inch) through suitable spade nozzles can be the quickest method. Often the dirt can be scooped off with a single pass over each area, the jet acting like a knife, and the quantity of water used can be kept quite small, since only short bursts are needed over each part. Again, it is desirable to protect areas below from run-off, and, of course, to ensure that windows are watertight.

Steam

There was a period when many cleaning specialists recommended steam, particularly for indoor use above wooden fittings; but since the development of other methods it is now seldom used, having too few advantages to justify the extra complications and cost. Steam can help to remove oil or paint; a steam kettle is the traditional way of removing layers of limewash from deeply recessed enrichments.

Chemical cleaning

In the early days many cleaning firms added chemicals to the water they used, because dirt could thereby be removed so much more quickly and therefore more cheaply. Much damage was done, and today the general rule is never to apply any chemical to stonework without a guarantee that all will be removed after the cleaning has been completed (a standard that no one in the trade has yet been able to reach). Under expert advice occasional exceptions to this prohibition may however be permissible. Here are some.

- Dilute hydrofluoric acid can be a very useful aid in the cleaning of sandstones and unpolished granites, but the method involves so many risks that it should only be used by experts. It can seriously burn or poison operatives, who must be supplied with full protection; it can leave unsightly iron stains in the stone unless every trace of acid is washed away, and it can contaminate unexpected objects such as scaffold boards, poles and footpaths. Moreover, the acid can etch glass, marble, polished granite or paving.

- Alabaster that is unpainted and not too dirty can be cleaned with cotton wool and a little water, but the alabaster must be kept well clear of any running water. Stubborn dirt that resists such very gentle treatment can be removed with a chemical soap diluted in white spirit, but such treatment can only be carried out safely by experts. Further particulars will be found in the British Standard Code of Practice referred to on pages 7–8.

- Cement splashes and lime incrustations can be removed with a dilute solution based on hydrochloric acid and applied after clean water, but unless the acid is washed off very thoroughly it may damage the stone.

- Fresh graffiti can usually be removed from masonry with water-rinsable solvents such as Polyclens, but longstanding disfigurements can be very hard to get off without risking serious damage to the stone. Places liable to repeated disfigurement can be protected by applying a chemical manufactured by Cementation Ltd and sold as Hydron. The presence of Hydron is almost invisible and graffiti subsequently painted on can be rubbed off very easily; but aerosol disfigurements are not dealt with so easily.

- Chemicals can also play a useful role in the removal of lichens and mosses. These are not nearly so harmful to stone as is often thought; in fact their main contribution to decay lies in their tendency to keep the surface of masonry damp at times when it would otherwise be dry. But some lichens do attack stone and others cause unsightly white patches. Formulations based on pentachlorphenol or tributyl tin oxide have proved very effective in removing such growths and yet are not injurious to stone. A long-lasting such formulation is at present marketed under the trade name of Murosol.

Dry air-abrasive

Such cleaning can be useful even on limestones – in places where water is likely to prove harmful or ineffective – and is in more general use for cleaning sandstones. It can, however, cause serious damage if used without suitable precautionary measures. Ordinary sands or other siliceous grits (such as flint) are rarely used now that the risks that operatives may develop silicosis have become appreciated. Non-siliceous grits can be equally efficient, though more expensive, and are made from various substances (such as iron or copper slags or even glass) reduced to many different grades of fineness, some of which produce sharper cuts and others a rougher 'buffing' effect. The coarseness of the grit and the size of nozzle used are crucial. A coarse grit can have devastating results on a soft stone and it is only too easy to take the sharpness off arrises; indeed, permanent damage can be caused by one moment of negligence. On most stones the finer the grit used the less damage is done, but on Kentish Rag coarse grit has unexpectedly been found to be preferable to fine. The choice of aggregate will be governed not only by cost and suitability as a cleaning agent but also by the overriding need to protect the health of operatives. Use of a cheap but dangerous abrasive may make it necessary to insist upon expensive equipment (such as positive pressure helmets), which can prove so clumsy that delicate work becomes impossible. Most expert cleaning firms are prepared to introduce controls on their equipment, which help the operatives to avoid damaging fragile detail or producing blotchy patches. For the cleaning of very precious objects see Chapter 10 (especially the sections on cleaning on pages 54 and 55), but there are many reasons why it is impracticable to apply such specialized techniques over large areas.

The spread of dry grit is so difficult to control and can be so objectionable that it should never be used on inhabited domestic property. Even where conditions are not so critical, every feasible precaution needs to be taken to protect operatives, the interior of the building, and adjoining paths and properties from airborne grit. Gutters and drains should be cleared daily. Treated areas should be washed down soon after grit blasting ceases but, even so, they may remain rather uniformly drab in appearance.

Damp air-abrasive

Such cleaning does not spread objectionable grit so widely, but it has its disadvantages. Operatives do not like it (nozzles block so easily); so the result may be uneven standards of workmanship, causing unsightly blotches at the end. An additional washing down operation is required after cleaning, and it is still necessary to provide the operatives with full protection.

Power tools

With the help of power tools such as carborundum disks dirt can be removed from recalcitrant places that have not been successfully cleaned by abrasive treatment. But their use must necessarily remove the surface of the stone to a greater depth than one could wish. Moreover, the use of power tools is likely to introduce patches of unsympathetic texture in the finished result. Such tools should never be used for cleaning or resurfacing medieval stonework without the specific consent of the architect, which should rarely (if ever) be given.

Poultice cleaning

Most of the foregoing summaries of cleaning methods mention the risks inherent in the use of such methods in unsuitable ways or on unsuitable materials. Cases will arise when the problems involved are so difficult that no normal cleaning method can produce a satisfactory result without causing damage – when, for example, the object to be cleaned is made of a very vulnerable material such as alabaster or has already decayed almost to the point of disintegration but still preserves its original shape, which yet has great artistic importance. Many such difficult problems can be solved by the temporary application of suitable poultices, but these are expensive and the problems involved are so complex that advice should always be sought from some skilled conservator.

Combinations of various methods

On many buildings the best results will be obtained by a combination of one or more of the above methods. Heavily sulphated crockets in exposed positions on Wells Cathedral were dissolved into mush in a couple of days by a simple method of water spray, which had amply proved its efficiency when used over a period of 40 years on plain ashlar built of the same Doulting stone; yet the simpler method remains eminently suitable for use on more durable surfaces that can take it safely.

Choice of the method most appropriate for each part will depend upon the following considerations:

Type and conditions of each surface

Sandstone or limestone? Exposed or sheltered? Ashlar or deeply undercut? Crumbly or hard condition? Precautions needed against penetration of damp or grit into interior?

Possibility of coordinating manpower

It may be possible to coordinate manpower in order to reduce time wasted in standing around. Both wet and dry cleaning can interfere with other trades working nearby, and vice versa. When wet and dry cleaning is carried out on adjacent areas the dry nozzles can get clogged by damp. With low-pressure water spraying much time can be spent waiting to shift the nozzle positions. Can arrangements be made for this to be done by masons working nearby on stone renewals?

Possible programming of work

Evaluation of the time needed to complete each process enables the work of each trade to be programmed economically in each area. Dry cleaning can be carried out in frosty weather.

General convenience

Likely delivery dates and interference with services inside the church, passers by or adjoining owners by splashing, drifting grit, or objectionable noise can all be considerations in deciding the choice of method that will be used.

Relative costs of different methods

chapter 5
Stone decay: types and causes

Before discussing stone repair it will be helpful to consider the main types of decay and their causes, and it should be realized from the start that all of them are either caused or encouraged by too much moisture. They can be classified under the following main headings.

Frost

In England frost does not damage stonework as often as is sometimes thought, its effects being chiefly seen in stone such as copings, which are liable to repeated freezing while very wet. It is the distribution of pore sizes within the stone that determines whether or not it is liable to frost damage. Two types of damage occur: stones that are exposed on three or more faces can suffer major fractures when cooled rapidly by freezing winds, because water in the stone is trapped by a casing of ice; whereas stones whose top surfaces only are cooled by freezing snow or by radiation loss to a night sky develop lens-shaped fractures on their top surfaces.

fig. 1
A limestone coping showing the characteristic decay caused by frost. The Grange, Alresford

© John Ashurst

Chemical attack

Some forms of stone decay are directly due to chemical action. Modern conditions have increased the quantities of carbon dioxide and sulphur dioxide in the air and, when these combine with water, they form an acid, which dissolves calcite in the stone. In consequence, the washed surfaces of durable limestones such as Portland will dissolve away slowly but steadily (whereas sheltered areas grow a hard black skin that develops blisters). On a siliceous limestone such as Reigate the dissolution of quite small amounts of the calcite that holds the sand together can release large grains, which is a principal reason for the poor weathering qualities of Reigate in polluted urban atmospheres.

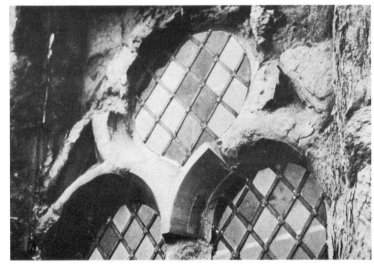

fig. 2
Window tracery showing pollution attack on the dolomitic cement binding of the stone particles, and repair work recording the original profiles. Bolsover Castle

© John Ashurst

Crystallization damage

Crystallization can cause physical damage as well as hastening chemical action and is the worst agent of decay, occurring characteristically in positions that receive occasional rain and then undergo fairly rapid drying and causing most damage in stones having a relatively large surface area per unit volume (such as delicate tracery or deeply cut mouldings and carvings). As the stone gets wetter, chemically laden moisture penetrates more deeply into the interior; as the stone dries out quickly the chemicals crystallize below the surface. The more often this cycle is repeated the greater will be the tendency for these crystals to grow and to create dangerously expansive forces. Sulphur dioxide from the atmosphere (product of the combustion of both coal and oil but not of natural gas) is one of these harmful chemicals; it combines with the calcium in a limestone to form crystals of calcium sulphate. Magnesium sulphate forms similarly in magnesian limestones. Parallel or worse interactions can occur from salts derived from the ground or other sources. Such reversible moisture movements are inevitable; the effects the associated chemical actions will have upon the stone depend upon its composition (sulphur from atmospheric sources does not harm most sandstones) and upon its pore structure. It has been shown that for several complex reasons the finer its pore structure the more vulnerable a stone will be to decay. Crystallization of this nature causes powdering and blistering in limestones, deep cavities in magnesian limestones and sandstones, and also attacks calcite in calcareous sandstones.[1]

Wind erosion

In countries like Egypt this can be a serious factor, but important damage from wind erosion is rare in England. The deep concave cavities of decay, characteristic of some sandstones and commonly attributed to wind erosion, are in fact normally due to differences in the rates at which salts crystallize in those parts of a stone that are exposed to wind in comparison with those parts that are sheltered. Extra exposure causes more evaporation and consequently encourages more salts to accumulate and crystallize.

Contour scaling

Superficial defects are liable to develop on some sandstones, extending over the exposed faces of each stone regardless of its bed. The apparently sound surface becomes hollow, then splits, and large patches 2–10 mm thick ultimately flake off, exposing powdering material beneath. We are told that this is due to pores in the crust becoming blocked with calcium sulphate, which sets up shear

fig. 3
Typical
superficial
scaling.
Tintern
Abbey

© John Ashurst

17

stresses owing to differences in moisture and thermal movement between the crust and the core behind it. In stones that are not calcareous, the main source of calcium may be lime mortar in the joints. This effect has been very noticeable at Tintern Abbey and the old Coventry Cathedral as well as at St David's Cathedral.

Bacteria

It has been demonstrated that bacteria and micro-organisms can have some harmful effects on stone. These discoveries were written up excitedly some five decades ago, but later researches seem to show that this form of decay rarely has sufficient importance to worry the non-specialist.

Mosses and lichens

Although they gain their chief importance as harmful agents by acting as reservoirs for extra water, they can also release chemicals strong enough to etch limestones and attack metal roof coverings.

Mason bees

A quaint hazard is provided by the mason bee, which is sometimes found in old stonework, living in tunnels it has bored into soft stones. It is, however, solitary and rare and the stone must be very soft. The chief anxiety of the human masons who find a mason bee will be as to its likely reaction when disturbed, and they may well have more cause for anxiety from ordinary bees that have swarmed into cavities found in wall cores, entering through defective joints. To deal effectively with angry bees the help of an expert bee-keeper may be needed.

Human error

There are many ways in which stone decay can be perpetrated by human error either at the design stage or during execution; only a few of them can be mentioned here.

- Some of the commonest design errors have been those that cause over-large concentrations of water in undesirable places by unfortunate arrangements for outlets, gutters or damp-proof courses. Failure to protect the top surfaces of overhanging courses can have much the same effect.

- In the transition from design to execution the choice of unsuitable stone can be disastrous. Finding a suitable stone is a more difficult problem now than it was half a century ago, since there are fewer stones to choose from. In this connection a special word is needed about placing limestones and sandstones close together in the same building. Calcium sulphate is harmful to many sandstones, and one obvious way to introduce the calcium with which sulphur can combine is to insert limestones in close proximity to sandstones. The dangers of doing this have been widely taken to heart, perhaps because it is one of the easiest lessons to learn from a textbook without waiting for practical experience. If limestones are placed above sandstones, water running down from the limestone can cause rapid deterioration in the sandstone below (though the run-off from sandstones does not harm limestones). Amongst many sad examples, St Stephen's, Rochester Row, Westminster, can be cited, where, between the wars, Portland stone repairs were inserted into a York stone building. (Such an arrangement can also be criticized aesthetically as being likely after weathering to create white spots in a black building.) But this warning does not apply to all mixtures of limestone and sandstone. Trouble will ensue only if the sandstone in question is prone to decay by calcium sulphate. Ever since the Middle Ages the walls of Great Malvern Priory have been built of many different stones, and stones inserted during the last 75 years have included the limestones Ham Hill, Bath, Guiting and Clipsham mixed with different tints of the sandstone Hollington; yet experts have stated that they could find no instance of decay caused by this admixture.

- Errors during execution start with laying stones on the wrong bed. With most stones the 'natural' bed of the stone as it is found in the quarry should be laid horizontally in the building. There is great temptation to ignore this when choosing stones for mullions, shafts and erect statues for which one would like to use stones that are taller than the maximum height of blocks available in the quarry. Stones should never be 'face bedded', that is with the natural bed laid vertical and parallel to the wall face: this can cause disintegration. In some special cases (such as arch voussoirs and cornices whose lower mouldings are undercut) 'joint bedding' is desirable, that is to say with the natural bed vertical and at right angles to the wall face.

- Iron was commonly used in masonry for dowels, cramps, tie-bars and gutters from the Middle Ages to the end of the nineteenth century and its rusting remains one of the major reasons why stones still split. During this century however the lesson has been well learnt by masons, but not so well by other trades.

- Immense harm has been done to stonework by pointing up the joints with too hard a mortar, a very general practice in the second half of the nineteenth century and still too prevalent today. Except where there are special indications to the contrary, joints should be pointed with mortar that is less dense than the adjoining stone, thus encouraging evaporation moisture to pass out through the mortar (which is renewable) rather than through the stone.[2]

chapter 6
Deciding the extent and nature of required repairs

When starting to work on a phased programme of stone repair it is well to remember the first principle of conservation, namely, to keep renewals down to the reasonable minimum. Wholesale renewal must do irreparable damage to the historical integrity of the structure. Sometimes it is unavoidable but, when that is so, the need for wholesale renewal may well amount to outright condemnation of the actions or inactions of earlier generations. If only they had carried out partial repairs while there was yet time, the continuing unity of the whole need never have been broken. It is worth noting that such cases present a strong warning of the dangers of doing too little, even though we are considering them in the context of the major warning of the dangers of doing too much. It seems reasonable to aim at treating in a durable manner all stones judged likely to suffer major dilapidation during the interval that may be expected to elapse before the next round of extensive stone repair is undertaken on that part of the building. What that expected interval will be must be a matter of opinion and will vary according to many factors, one of which will be accessibility; on low aisles an average interval of 25–30 years has been deemed reasonable, but on high towers the equivalent figure might well be 75 years and on tall spires more again.[1]

What is meant by 'treating decaying stonework in a durable manner' will also be influenced by the nature of the building in question. A rustic building constructed of rough rubble will need very different treatment from one built of finely tooled ashlar between crisply moulded dressings. Above all, the philosophies appropriate to ruins are different from those that should be applied to buildings in active use. In a ruin, every original stone should in principle be conserved in position to the last possible moment; but a church in use should be helped to maintain its traditional conception and character. There are times when stones that have been renewed following the old details can hand on the building's message better than the mouldering originals. In the present generation we deplore the Victorian tendency to remove 'debased fifteenth-century accretions' in favour of presumed reconstructions of an original thirteenth-century design. We give value to all stages in the development of each building. We are also prepared to admit that the practical modern needs of a building in use should be given fair weight when they conflict with the demands of antiquarian purity. Pressed too far, these last may condemn a building to sterility.

It is worth pointing out that the last two paragraphs (as well as others in this guide) have been aimed chiefly at the renewal of stonework designed in the Gothic styles. Somewhat different criteria can sometimes be appropriate when dealing with classical buildings, where the scale is large but the surface detail simple. In some such cases the integrity of the whole elevation may deserve to be considered as important as the integrity of the historical stones out of which it was built.

Broad decisions as to the extent of stone repair need to be taken at an early stage so that the recommended programme can be costed, but they should remain subject to review at various stages as the amount of available information increases. A detailed survey will be needed at the start of each contract, and the architect will be wise to ask a knowledgeable mason to accompany him so that as wide an experience as possible can be drawn upon while decisions are being reached. One possible basis for such decisions is to aim at including suitable treatment for every stone deemed likely to develop major defects before the next occasion when a programme of extensive stone repair is likely to be mounted for that particular area (see page 21). Decisions are best recorded both on paper and on the stone in question. The architect is responsible for deciding what stone repair should be included in the initial contract and what extra percentage should be added provisionally to cover further needs, which are bound to be revealed as the work proceeds. To keep abreast of such variations, the architect should repeatedly revise the survey by stages as the work proceeds (particularly after cleaning has been completed). Taking the mason's advice, the architect may be called upon to decide jointing details and may well find it a duty to restrain a mason's too great longing for detailed perfection. It is not desirable that every stone on an old building be made as good as new.[2]

Something should also be said about the importance of record-keeping, before we pass to consideration of different methods of conservation. It has long been realized that the preparation of measured elevations and the stone-by-stone surveys they make possible are most helpful both in the early preparation stages of stone repair programmes and during the progress of contracts for such repairs. During the last decade, however, the realization has also spread that almost equal importance should be attached to the preparation at the end of each contract of record drawings, recording not what was planned but what was actually carried out. If such record drawings can be lodged in suitable places where they will be both safe and readily accessible, the future will benefit. Today's architects and archaeologists often wish that their predecessors had preserved such information.

All measured elevations had to be prepared by hand in previous generations and in many architects' offices skilled craftsmen were available until 1939 with experience in drawing complicated Gothic detail. Contracts today can rarely be provided with elevations measured and drawn by hand to the best Victorian standards. This is partly because of the expense involved but also because of time delays. In simple cases, plain or rectified photography can provide some assistance without great cost, but photography is subject to severe limitations, and photogrammetric elevations are being increasingly used. Their expense has often been proved to be justified, for they are superior to hand-measured drawings in some respects. The best result of all is a photogrammetric drawing that has been expertly revised on site by hand.[3]

As a sideline in the business of leaving records, several experienced architects recommend the practice of incising the date on new stones that have been inserted into old buildings. Confirmatory evidence of this kind can help considerably in later generations. Some architects also encourage masons to cut their own small mason marks on stones they have worked, thus reviving medieval practice.[4]

Masons should be instructed to take their templates from medieval mouldings wherever possible rather than from modern repairs; and a valuable extension of the record-keeping process will be gained if these templates can be preserved and safely stored at the end of the

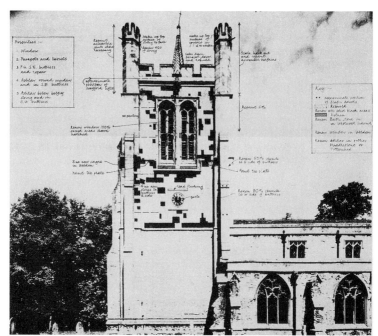

fig. 4
The use of a photograph to give clear instructions to the mason. Haslingfield, All Saints'

contract. At least in the case of large repair contracts on important cathedrals, that should not prove to be an impossible counsel of perfection.

In recent years there have been several moves to establish what amounts to a new discipline of field (as distinct from museum) conservators with special training in old and modern methods of preserving building materials that have special artistic or historic value. They will be referred to frequently in subsequent sections. Here, it is relevant to stress that conservators who work with stone can only gain by absorbing as many traditional masons' skills as possible. Advantage should be taken of every opportunity to encourage masons and conservators to work together.

chapter 7

Methods of repairing existing stonework

We now have to consider various ways of prolonging the life
of ageing stonework that does not yet need partial or complete
renewal.

Repointing

Unsuitable or defective pointing of the joints in stonework can
have a profound effect upon both appearance and durability.
Aesthetically, a good general rule is that the pointing itself should
never attract more attention than the stones it both joins and
separates; pointing can draw too much attention to itself by its
colour, texture or ability to throw or receive shadows. The
importance of this rule increases as the stones become smaller in
size and the joints occupy a larger proportion of the whole wall
face. But pointing can also have very practical effects on the life of
adjoining stones. Too open, it can allow water to stream into the
interior and plants to root and flourish. Too hard but broken at
frequent intervals by hair cracks, it can still admit large quantities
of wind-driven rain, yet retard the outward passage of the same
moisture through evaporation, causing the wall core to degenerate
into a sponge-like reservoir. Too dense a mortar can exaggerate
the build-up of harmful crystals in stones that are softer than the
mortar (as already explained on pages 3 and 20). Too rich a lime
content in mortar used for pointing sandstones can even start
decay round the edges of the stones, a minor example of the process
explained on page 19. Soft mortar pointing, however, will encourage
evaporation to take place through itself rather than through the
stone, and it is better that mortar should perish than stone.

Craftsmen not infrequently fail to cut out existing defective pointing
sufficiently deeply; 18 mm should normally be the minimum, and
greater depths may well be needed. When internal cavities are thus

exposed the opportunity should be taken to grout them solid, and it is often good practice to saw or disk defective coping joints right out. But care is needed to avoid damaging stone arrises with any tool whether disk, saw or hammer and chisel.[1]

Great variety is possible in the choice of materials used for repointing, and research followed by the preparation of several trial panels may often be needed to find the most suitable selections and mixes for different positions; mixes mentioned here must be regarded only as suggestions found useful in general practice, which often means that they can be specified for use by small contractors without experience in obtaining or using unusual materials. On this basis, cement–lime–sand mixes are still commonly specified for use by general building contractors, the lime being hydrated lime previously run into putty and the sand mixed with stone dust or grit and evenly graded up to 4 mm diameter. A 1:1:6 mix is often used in exposed positions, as well as during wintry weather for external work generally, but otherwise a weaker 1:2:8 mix marries better to old masonry. Similar results can be obtained more easily by direct mixes of 'masonry cement' and sand, treating 1:5 as equivalent to the above 1:1:6 and 1:6 as equivalent to 1:2:8. The use of one of these cement–lime–sand mixes is desirable in all cases where there is reason to fear that lime mortar may be causing decay in adjoining sandstones, and an effort should be made in such cases to avoid joints exceeding 10 mm in width. But recent work provides increasing evidence that mixtures containing no Portland cement can still be used with advantage today for pointing many limestones. The mix of 1 part of hydraulic lime to 2–1 parts of sand was used successfully in the earlier years of this century. Hydraulic lime is no longer easily obtained, but a lime mortar made with hydrated lime putty can be given some hydraulic set by mixing in finely ground brick dust or a sulphur-free pulverized fuel ash (PFA), both of which have what is known as a 'pozzolanic effect'. Finally, colour matching is important. It is better obtained not by adding pigments but by the mixing of suitable cements, limes, sands and brick dusts (PFA may be black). See also pages 31–3.[2]

Great importance attaches to very thorough wetting of stones before repointing and to keeping them sufficiently damp thereafter to prevent the new mortar setting too rapidly. The mortar (particularly lime mortar) must be well pressed in but, to reduce the development of superficial cracks or laitance, the surface should be disturbed after the set has begun by being brushed or rubbed over with sacking or a wooden tool used in a conscious attempt to reproduce the original finish (avoiding the struck joints so commonly introduced during the last 100 years). This advice can only be followed if the work is so organized that pointing stops quite early in the afternoon, leaving time to brush it off before the end of the day. The surface of adjoining stones should be kept clean; in order to attain this, it is often advantageous to recess new pointing slightly more than was done originally.[3]

Removal of harmful iron

The lesson has been well learned nowadays that iron embedded in masonry is likely to damage the surrounding stones by the expansion that takes place during rusting; nevertheless, it is well to remember that this process can be very slow. Unnecessarily wholesale replacement of all iron can be very damaging to antiquity. Some early wrought iron has hardly rusted at all even after being fully exposed to the weather for centuries (interesting examples have been noted on Curry Mallet church tower). Moreover, in the best-designed works it has been the practice for many centuries to protect buried iron with lead sheathing, which sometimes remains effective. It may therefore be wise to limit replacements of iron to those places judged likely to cause trouble before the next round of stone repair to that part of the building (see Chapter 6, first para.). The most difficult decisions can occur where medieval walls have been refaced in ashlar in the eighteenth century, when it was common practice to use iron to cramp every stone to its neighbour.

Slate or even pebbles have long been used for small dowels between adjacent stones and these are particularly valuable if it proves necessary to renew copings in precast stone, which shrinks more than the natural material. At the beginning of the twentieth century bronze and later the stronger delta-metal were used instead of iron for tie-rods or girdles round spires in the realization that galvanized iron is untrustworthy. The price of delta-metal is now so high however that its place has been taken by stainless steel, since steel alloys have been developed that really do not rust.[4]

Special considerations arise in the case of iron bars across windows, commonly known as ferramenta and usually placed outside the glazing. Originally, they were erected to keep out thieves (as in the Wells Cathedral undercroft) and to support lead glazing. The first of these purposes has relevance today, but the second rarely has, because lead glazing is now usually fixed to internal rustless saddle-bars. The chief value of external ferramenta now is in the important contribution they can make to maintaining the external unity of a Gothic church in texture and scale; they should never be removed before careful balance has been struck between their aesthetic advantages and practical disadvantages. Continuous iron bars are often found running right across multi-light windows at springing level. These should be cut at every mullion or, if necessary, replaced in non-rusting metal. The rusting ends of other saddlebars also damage stonework and various efforts have been made to protect the ends better. One method used during the last 50 years has been to file bright the ends that will be buried and then dip them in neat cement grout (instead of paint) before they are set in lime mortar. A more recent suggestion has been to use epoxy mortar for pointing up the mortice holes. Sometimes enough money has been available to pay for welding bronze or stainless steel tips to the ends of interesting old bars.[5]

Protections over projecting members

The upper surfaces of projecting labels and string courses in Gothic buildings – and cornices in classical buildings – tend to get saturated much more readily than surrounding stonework and consequently decay faster if made of soft stone. Their useful life can be prolonged by superimposing some suitable protection, often of lead, preferably finished with its outer edge neatly trimmed to form an inconspicuous drip. Quite apart from the question of stone decay, most walls tend to stay cleaner if their faces can be protected from local concentrations of water running off surfaces above.[6]

Superficial treatments

Chemical preservatives

One of the first questions an architect is often asked after recommending an expensive programme of stone repair is, 'Can't we make the present stones last longer by applying some stone preservative?' For over 100 years people have been trying out schemes for doing just this, but most of them have in the long run proved to be more harmful than doing nothing while others have had no appreciable effect. Some of the dangers inherent in all chemical applications have already been indicated in the section on chemical cleaning on pages 9–10. A principal risk is to convert the surface of stone into an impermeable crust, which does nothing to alleviate the more deep-seated processes of decay and only holds them back temporarily until their pressure increases sufficiently to burst off the surface crust. Despite specious claims still put forward for the preservative qualities of chemical applications to stonework, the best advice in most cases is '**Don't**; it will be money wasted'.

Silicone water repellants

There are, however, occasions when the superficial application of silicone water repellants can benefit masonry built of stones so laminated or porous that repointing alone cannot make them watertight. It is important to select a repellant that will permit water vapour to evaporate from the interior even though it stops liquid water entering the surface. The effect of such silicones does not last many years, but it can provide a very valuable respite, particularly when the core of a thick wall has been saturated through and through so that a couple of heavy storms can cause water to ooze through into the interior. This was the case with the tower of Hawkridge on Exmoor, built of laminated and (at the time) badly pointed local stone, and also with the tower of Hawkley in Hampshire, down whose very porous stone walls all the water off the spire streamed owing to a design fault. The interiors of both towers were green with mould. But once the first tower had been repointed and water off the spire of the second had been kept away from the walls below, superficial applications of waterproofers allowed the cores to dry out enough to enable the seasonal evaporation of water vapour to balance out the diminished intake of storm water. The internal green moulds were removed and did not recur. Silicone water repellants can be usefully applied to the external surfaces of mullions and traceries that are decaying internally (as often happens with magnesian limestones). Silicone water repellants should be applied when stonework is as dry as possible. Useful advice will be found in BRE Digest No. 125(January 1971), which divides such silicones into three classes, A for sandstones and B or C for limestones (of which C will behave better in damp conditions).[7]

Lime water on limestones

Before discussing the use of lime water for consolidating softened stonework it is important to make clear that this does **not** imply covering the stones with what is often called limewash – an opaque layer of white or tinted material such as has been recommended by one school of thought since the early twentieth century. We are now talking about the application of water with a high lime content that hopefully looks just like ordinary water, without showing any signs of the scum that forms so quickly on the surface of lime water as soon as it is exposed to the air. The theory is to return to the stones some of the calcium they have lost through incipient decay. It is over 50 years since Mr W. A. Wheeler, then an observant mason apprentice, noticed that the last action each day of masons engaged on inserting new stones into decaying windows was to clean their brushes and the cills by slapping on water out of the buckets they had been using for mixing lime mortar and he noticed later on that the stones so slapped seemed usually to grow harder. This led him to experiment with deliberate applications of water with a high lime content to various parts of Wells Cathedral, and he obtained results that were thought still to have been beneficial 25 years later, in that the still satisfactory surfaces could no longer be dented with a fingernail as before. But later examinations seemed to show that the improvements observed were due not to the lime applied but to other causes. Perhaps the evaporation that can follow periodic washing may have helped to remove harmful chemicals from near the stone surface. Nevertheless, these investigations at Wells Cathedral did not lead to condemnations of the use of lime water for strengthening softened limestone but rather to support for its use in more efficient ways, following the techniques pioneered by Professor Robert Baker. The lime content of the water that is transferable into the stone can be increased to 4 per cent by keeping the lime water in collapsible polythene bags from which air can easily be excluded. Applications should continue until the stone will absorb no more: between 30 and 40 operations are often needed, the water being applied through a fine spray at intervals over a period of several days.[8]

Resin grouting of fine cracks

There are many reasons why stones that seem otherwise quite sound can develop fine cracks, and these may be so fine that they cannot be stopped either by repointing or by grouting with lime (or cement). In the old days there were rarely more than three options available: renewing the stone in question, widening the crack with a chisel (which would be unthinkable with sculpture) or doing nothing until the defect grew so much worse as to become unacceptable. Such fissures can now be consolidated with low viscosity (that is, runny) or thixotropic epoxide resins put deliberately in selected spots. Necessary preliminary cleaning is first carried out and small quantities of plasticine are applied temporarily to confine the liquid within the desired areas. If runny resins are to be used, all surfaces at risk below should be coated temporarily with latex so that run-offs can be peeled away easily (thixotropic resins should not run). The resin, which is supplied in two packs, is then mixed and injected with a hypodermic syringe, extra tamping being possible in wider places before curing has advanced too far. These resins can be used on damp stone, but care is advisable not to form a continuous damp-proof course behind any part of the stone surface. Repairs of this nature obviously need expert handling; they have been carried out most successfully by the Directorate of Ancient Monuments and Historic Buildings (DAMHB) of the Department of the Environment at Tintern Abbey and at Wells Cathedral, among other places.

Minor surface repairs

Though major renewals of defective masonry will be dealt with in Chapter 8, we are concerned here with the many occasions when there is need to make up or bring forward small areas of stone as inconspicuously as possible. There are often good reasons why such work should, if possible, be entrusted to labour already on site, without introducing specialist assistance. This brings us to one of the most potentially useful sections of this guide, since we now have to consider innovations that have found their way into general practice during the last five years. Intensive experiment and research carried out over many years by the DAMHB and by the Building Research Establishment at Garston and others have enlarged our understanding of the problems of stone decay and introduced changes both into current practice and into the theories that underlie it. A more coordinated view has been taken of the various methods desirable in pointing work (normally carried out by general contractor's staff), in plastic stone repair (normally done by specialist contractors) and in the conservation of irreplaceable foliage carving and statuary (which should only be entrusted to highly skilled conservators); and it has been urged that all are concerned with the same problems in different degree and that no firm lines should be drawn between them. It has been suggested that the term 'plastic stone' should be dropped as misleading and that all attempts to build up the surface of individual stones should be referred to as 'mortar repairs', whether carried out by masons or conservators. We have on balance preferred to retain here the old separate headings familiar in the architectural profession and building trade, but we would point out that the distinction that really matters between the simplest and the most complex of these operations is which of them can be safely entrusted to craftsmen employed in the normal trade and which of them should be reserved for specialist experience. On a rising scale of expertise we are here concerned with the border-line, where the highest capabilities of general labour should give way to specialist dexterity, and the aim of this subsection is to give advice that might help to move that border slightly upward, so that more firms and craftsmen in the general trade can be safely entrusted with a larger proportion of the highly skilled operations that the stonework of so many churches needs.[9]

Most architects engaged on quinquennial repairs are all too familiar with the contract that includes no new masonry despite a need still to make up odd little corners of medieval stones. When it was wholly impracticable to call in a distant specialist for so small a task, one used only to be able to ask the general contractor to do his best, and hope that the next connoisseur who saw the result would not label it a botch. Even on the simpler matter of pointing, most architects can remember cases where the contractor has genuinely tried to follow the specification and yet the result has been far from perfect. A conservator would have achieved far better results; but a builder who has no experience of using many varieties of sand with different colours and grain sizes, and who is working within a fixed contract price, cannot be forced to spend days on obtaining samples and experimenting with them, as the conservator would. Moreover the architect knows that his own standard specification represents only an average of experience. If cost were no object, the result on any one building could almost certainly be improved by extensive initial experiment. What help can the latest developments offer?[10]

There is nothing new in the continuing emphasis upon matching existing work as closely as possible consistent with permanence, upon avoiding feather-edges, with no coat more than 18 mm thick, and upon the importance of thorough wetting of existing work, both before and after. The experts now however advise us to use softer and rather different mixes than have been normal in recent practice, and to take greater care in their preparation and matching. Before starting even minor reconstitution of stonework, samples of alternative mortars should be prepared and trial experiments should be made to determine which materials and quantities will produce the closest match after setting and drying off. Thus no rigid specification can be recommended even for matching stone from a named quarry, but the following general guide may help in selecting the initial mix from which experiments should proceed by way of variants.[11]

Mix 1 part of 'lime', which should be mature lime putty, with between 2 and 3 parts of 'sand' which should be a mixture of stone dust matching the adjoining stones and sand of suitable grain size and colour. The proportions of stone dust and sand can vary and the sand should be selected (and perhaps mixed) from various colours and sieved to varying degrees of coarseness as may be appropriate for the particular building. It is advantageous to mix this 'lime' and 'sand' together into 'coarse stuff' as long before use as possible, provided it is kept damp. To this coarse stuff add 10 per cent of 'brickdust' finely ground from clay bricks of suitable colour. This addition must not be made until the last moment, following normal practice for cement.[12]

If a firm that specializes in reconstructed or plastic stone is already on site, then the problems of effecting minor plastic repairs will be easier, because the firm will probably have experimented with various sands already and its men will have wider experience of the techniques required. Nevertheless a careful watch over techniques and execution will still be needed. Fine buildings have been ruined by firms claiming to be specialists in plastic stone. Further details will be found in the section on plastic stone in Chapter 8.

The interior of Westminster Hall provides a special example of the value of using epoxy resins in the conservation of stone surfaces. Large quantities of water had to be used to put out the fire that broke out in 1974 at the north end, with the result that the internal surfaces of the stone walls were first heated and then drenched with cold water. The wall in question was eleventh century, faced with typical Norman ashlar with rectangular stones varying in size both vertically and horizontally. A thin superficial layer of stone split off from the bulk of the stone behind. In the worst instances the superficial layer fragmented but amazingly most of the pieces were saved from the debris and could be fitted together again like a jigsaw puzzle. Many other stones appeared at first sight to be in good condition but sounded hollow when tapped and were ready to fall. Using traditional techniques, the only sound course would have been to cut back large areas and reface with new ashlar, but under the supervision of the architects of DAMHB it has proved possible to preserve the original Norman tooled face apparently untouched. Deep holes were drilled into the intersections of the joints, that is, at every corner of each affected stone. The holes were grouted up with epoxy resin into which glass-reinforced polyester pins were pressed, thus forcing the soft uncured resin sideways into splits and cavities where it provided sufficient holding pads to stick the loose surfaces firmly on again. Finally the face was repointed in traditional manner, with most convincing results.

Similar methods were used for a different purpose to strengthen a twelfth-century capital in the south arcade of Compton church. The arcade is built of chalk or clunch, and one scalloped capital, carved out of a single huge stone, was splitting. The ends of the cracks were marked and dated at intervals over a period of five years, recording the extent and rate of progressive movement, and tapping began to reveal hollow areas indicating that chunks might fall out.

No cracks had however developed either in the cylindrical pier below the capital or in the round arches above it; so that the trouble was clearly localized in that one stone, probably caused by uneven bedding. Traditional wisdom demanded the renewal of the whole cap, but (apart from the cost of shoring and underpinning) chalk of that size is unobtainable, and any modern replacement would have clashed badly with the chalky whiteness of that axe-cut arcade. In 1974 the original capital was successfully strengthened by grouting cracks (with the same epoxy resin as had been used in Westminster Hall) and then threading two glass fibre rods horizontally through the capital in each direction. One unexpected problem was the difficulty of using a diamond drill to bore 12 mm-diameter holes 1 m-long through soft chalk: compacted dust stopped the drills.

Maintenance of general harmony

Before leaving consideration of methods of conserving the surfaces of existing stones it may be helpful to recapitulate some general points. In every aspect of good conservation one aim should always be to retain the aesthetic harmony of the old building, minimizing the patchy effect of piecemeal repairs. But this aim is in constant conflict with limitations imposed by lack of materials or finance, and compromise is often necessary.

The desirability of avoiding patchiness applies particularly to repointing. Even when it is carried out under a sympathetic specification, few things can do more to destroy the unity of an elevation than dotting streaks and blotches of new pointing at random over a wide expanse of wall. The bad effects of doing this in the interests of economy are most obvious when the wall is faced with small rubble stones, or flint cobbles, or widely pointed brickwork. A small patch of clean pointing looks blatant in a dirty ashlar wall. Such undesirable contrasts can be lessened either by extensive cleaning or by extending the areas of new pointing to coincide with whole units in the architectural design.

Help in the solution of such problems can be found by either cleaning the old or colouring down the new and cleaning, in particular, should also be spread over purposeful areas. In the long term it is best to achieve unity by cleaning dirt off old stones rather than by toning new stones down artificially; but on the exterior (and provided one is prepared to brave the hostile comments of the enemies of any change, who are always most observant immediately after completion when contrasts are most stark) the need to clean the older parts of patched elevations merely to achieve aesthetic unity diminishes rapidly as our British weather softens the brightness of new materials. When the central tower of Bangor Cathedral was raised in 1967 the new White Hollington contrasted strongly with the black stonework below. Ten years later it was hard to pick out the dividing line. But internally the dilemma may be more acute. At the turn of the century Sir Aston Webb built a new triforium round the apse of St Bartholomew-the-Great in the City. He is believed to have used tea to tone it to match surrounding stonework. Sixty years later the whole interior was cleaned, but it was impossible to remove the tea stain, which still after a further 20 years stands out as a brown patch.

Sentiment should not be allowed to influence this question too far where many medieval churches are concerned. People talk too glibly about retaining the 'original' effect. For 250 years after the Reformation the interiors of most English churches were whitewashed; then, for 100 years, the prevalent fashion was to strip skimmings and plaster off both internal and external stonework, which had in fact been designed to be covered. Now many critics do not realize that a facade like the west front of Wells Cathedral was at first fully tinctured like a gigantic reredos and that the ashlar of countless medieval churches was limewashed over, both inside and out, with false joints painted on, bearing small relationship to the structural joints below. Some will remember being disturbed by such false jointing reproduced mechanically by Butterfield all over the interior of St Cross near Winchester and now mercifully removed. Our eyes have grown to appreciate the beauties of bare stonework textured by the irregularities of medieval tooling; the medieval builders would not have agreed, but few people now would follow their practice.[13]

chapter 8
Choice of materials for replacements

Natural stone

There are many occasions when conservation of existing stonework is no longer possible and replacement becomes essential. Until half a century ago natural stone was almost the only obvious material to use in good quality repairs even though eighteenth-century builders did sometimes insert patches of brickwork (which are now considered to add quaint interest to their surroundings). There used to be an immense number of natural stones available from which to choose, and many masons were skilled in recognizing them. Judgement of the qualities of stones rested not on scientific tests, but on individual experience. The truth of the then commonly held view that stones weather best if kept in their own locality depended largely upon the fact that most local masonry firms were known personally to the quarry foremen, who would not sell inferior stones to such frequent and friendly customers. Conditions now are very different.

Selection of type of stone

When new stones have to be inserted into an old building today it is common to find that the particular type of stone used there is no longer obtainable. Sometimes the original quarry has been worked out or is unknown; just as often, similar stone is known still to exist in the ground but the quarry has been closed, because demand for many building stones is now so small and so intermittent in Britain that the processes of quarrying can no longer be made to pay. There is more scientific advice available about natural building stones than ever before, but it is often difficult to link it to the practicalities of the particular case. In a subject so full of detailed facts, most of which will be irrelevant to the needs of any particular building, the most helpful course for a short publication will be merely to sketch the general field and then indicate where further information can be obtained. We start therefore with an outline of the kind of question that needs answering when searching for the best kind of natural stone to use for repairs to a particular church:

- First it is desirable to identify the type (or types) of stone previously used on the building and the district from which it came. An architect will often find that he can get help in this most easily from an experienced mason or builder and that confirmation can be obtained by sending (or, better still, taking) a sample to the Geological Museum.[1]
- A suitably matching stone needs then to be chosen, often a very difficult task since so many quarries in this country have closed down. Similar stone may well be very short-lived under modern conditions or, indeed, be completely unobtainable. The sources of available building stone vary only too quickly and are too complicated for enumeration here. Useful lists will be found in that invaluable manual, *Stone in Building*, and in the latest edition of the *Natural Stone Directory* (see Bibliography). Advice as to anticipated longevity can be obtained from the Building Research Establishment, Garston.
- Are there choices of bed, texture and tint available in the quarry?
- How durable can the stone be expected to be in the proposed position?
- What maximum depth of bed is normally available?
- What is the cost and likely delay in delivery?
- If no suitable replacements are available in England, can acceptable alternatives be obtained from abroad (usually France at present)?

Quality control of stone delivered and fixed

Stone, being a natural material, is subject to infinite variations and constant vigilance is needed in quality control. The key to success lies in the closest liaison between architect and experienced mason, and this can be buttressed further if the mason can be persuaded to establish personal contact with the quarry foreman. Some stones are much more easily worked (and are said to prove more durable) if they are worked before their natural quarry sap has evaporated.[2]

Economy in working stone

Stone repairs using the old labour-intensive methods have become so expensive and so wasteful of skills now comparatively rare that it is in the interests of the buildings themselves – as well as of the skilled masonry trade – to lower costs and increase productivity by introducing modern methods into the craft whenever that can be done without blatant harm to the finished product. Nothing written here is intended to detract from the value of hand-tooling for the production of textured surfaces; but large savings in time can be achieved if masons can be persuaded to use machinery of all sorts for reducing stones to within 2 mm of their intended contours. Even deep thirteenth-century mouldings can be produced successfully in this way. Owing to the high capital cost of the larger machines, most stones are worked more economically in the firm's yard than on site; but a word of warning is justified here. Piecing the most difficult stones into an existing building can become so complicated that success can only be achieved if they are worked on site, so that the mason can pass backwards and forwards between stone and building as he shapes the stone.[3]

Architectural control

As well as controlling the extent of the stone renewals he is prepared to authorize, the architect should also encourage the maximum sympathy between new work and old. Some churches were built using stones of different tints, in which case care is needed not only in the selection of varieties but also in their relative disposition. Joint positions and the size of stones used should be controlled to avoid noticeable change in scale; this is one of the factors that often makes it desirable to avoid piecing in too many small corners. Control of joint widths is also desirable. Though some say that the old widths should be reproduced exactly, in fact one new stone inserted into an area of old facing will weather more quickly into its surroundings if the joints round it are widened slightly; moreover, it is reasonable to postulate a general rule for most Gothic buildings that new ashlar joints should never be made so fine that they cannot be repointed.[4]

Piecing in: traditional method

When following traditional methods of piecing new stones into existing facings, the depth of the stones is varied to achieve an efficient bond, with a minimum thickness of 100 mm. Great care should be taken to pack and grout solid all cavities behind the facing; but the proportion of cement in the grout should be kept low where no important structural weakness is involved. Policy for mullions depends upon what treatment is suitable for the glazing. If the interior of the mullion is sound and the glazing can remain in position, decayed external stones are normally cut back to the glass line (sometimes called 'half-soling'), each replacement stone being dowelled through to the old stone behind (though a long vertical joint more than about 1.8 m high is considered risky without a through bonder). Monolithic mullions provide one of the few instances where it is good practice to alter previous jointing methods. Mullions should never be end-bedded; extra joints should be introduced where needed to make natural bedding possible and, in medieval buildings, such joints should be irregularly spaced.

Piecing in: superficial method

A new method of piecing in has however been introduced at Carlisle Cathedral, with considerable saving on initial cost. Since only their external faces had decayed, sandstone clerestory windows were refaced with hand-tooled natural stones only 50 mm thick that were both dowelled on and stuck with a resin mortar, which acts as a vertical damp-proof course. The risks of forming vertical damp-proof courses close behind the front fillet were no doubt considered. All the templates were retained as a precaution against possible failure later.

Plastic stone

Modern methods of masonry repair using reconstructed or plastic stone have now been in active use for over 50 years, long enough to show that while some of them can be disastrous others can be claimed as acceptable on a 'permanent' basis. Though it must be admitted that a few opponents remain resolutely unconvinced, the reasonable conclusion seems now to be, first, that only the best methods applied by experienced craftsmen should be admissible and, secondly, that the best plastic stone is superior to natural stone in some conditions and inferior in others. The arguments for and against need to be carefully weighed.

Advantages

- When only parts of stones have decayed, repair using plastic stone often enables more original surface to be retained than would be possible if new natural stones were inserted. This can be a valuable asset when interesting original detail is involved.
- The vibrations caused by cutting away are liable to damage fragile surroundings, and less cutting is necessary for plastic repair than for wholesale renewal.
- When repairing decayed arches the use of plastic stone may make it possible to avoid cutting out whole voussoirs. The cost of expensive centring and shoring can sometimes be saved in this way.
- The insertion of a few new stones into an area that has generally weathered back can produce disturbing contrasts and shadows. It is sometimes desirable to 'distress' the new work for the sake of harmony; this is seldom possible with natural stone, easy with plastic.
- Although plastic stone is more expensive than natural stone volume for volume, the cost of plastic stone repair is usually less than that of natural repair because the volume is so much smaller. Sometimes such savings can be considerable, but it is necessary to be very careful to ensure that they are not made by

omitting precautions that are essential if plastic stone is to be an acceptable material.

Disadvantages

- In especially exposed places even the best plastic stone will not last as long as durable natural stone; moreover, its appearance tends to become less attractive after being exposed to the weather, whereas most natural stones improve.[5]
- New plastic stone is liable to develop defects (as for example crazing) or to become unsatisfactory in various ways (such as drabness in colour) unless the operatives are prepared to make frequent adjustments in their techniques as the work proceeds. Much depends upon the skill and judgement of the individual operative and upon the time his firm will allow him to spend upon such adjustments while he is working within the financial limits of an accepted tender. The drabness of extensive plastic repairs can, however, be largely avoided if plastic and natural insertions are mixed together.
- Opponents of plastic stone reiterate that it is a 'fake'; but so too are other materials we are glad to use in suitable positions.

Techniques

Plastic stone has been prepared using various materials and many methods. Here we shall only describe the cement/lime mix that is the method of which both architects and operatives have had the widest and longest experience during the last 50 years.

- Decayed stone should be dressed back till a sound face is reached and to a minimum depth of 25 mm with no feather-edges permitted. Experience on Doulting stone at Wells Cathedral indicates that at this stage it can be advantageous (but expensive) to treat the fresh surface thus exposed with lime water as described in the section on limestones in Chapter 7 (pages 30–31).
- Adequate keying is obtained either by cutting dovetailed slots or by drilling holes at close centres. If the repair is deeper than 50 mm, loops of 8 gauge copper wire are fixed into some of the holes. The wire should never come closer than 20 mm to the finished surface.
- The materials and mixes used for plastic stone need to be adjusted experimentally to suit particular places with just as

much care as has been recommended for pointing on pages 25–6. The final result should always be weaker and more porous than the stone being repaired. Remembering that most natural stones vary in tint within the same quarry and that plastic stone tends to weather into dull uniformity, it is good practice to have two or three mixes of slightly varying tints available simultaneously for use on adjoining stones. The desired tints are obtained by mixing in varying (but small) quantities of specially chosen sands or stone dust. The proportion in which these materials are used should be adjusted on and within each particular building to suit not only the colour but also the porosity of the existing stone, and the following average mix is put forward only as an initial proposal, which should be amended to suit local conditions.

Stone dust prepared from stone similar to the surrounding work	5½ parts,
Sands selected and mixed as above	2½ parts,
Lime (hydrated or other suitable)	1 part,
Cement (wholly or mainly white)	1 part.

This gives an overall mix of 8:1:1 which can be varied slightly as explained.

- After saturating the exposed faces with water from a soft brush, the new plastic stone is worked on, built up to the desired profile (in more than one coat where necessary) and finished with a wooden float. To avoid crazing, it must always be left with a slightly rough surface. The plastic is applied separately to each original stone, without contact with adjoining plastic.

- After the initial set, final texturing is applied with any suitable wooden (never steel) tool. In formal work, tooling can be simulated by drawing a comb across the half-set surface. Informal results can be obtained by heavy texturing and softening of mouldings, choosing the right moment to use rough-edged tools to abrade the surface. Fir cones were used at Pulborough church in an attempt to simulate weathered Wealden sandstone.[6]

- Uncured plastic (that which has not yet developed its full strength) must be carefully protected from the sun by means of damp sacks. After the final set has been completed, it is possible

fig. 6a

fig. 6b
Mortar
repair used
to simulate
unstable
and heavily
weathered
Sussex
sandstone:
a before
and *b* after.
Pulborough,
St Mary's

© Stuarts
Granolithic Ltd

to work the surface with normal masonry techniques, though it
is a delicate operation.

- At least a week must be allowed to elapse before open joints are
  pointed solid in the normal way.

Appraisal

Some old buildings are built of stone for which no close match is obtainable amongst natural building stones available today. When only a few small patches need replacement on a large wall face, the use of plastic stone can provide an inconspicuous solution to a very difficult problem.

In the interests of durability, it is wise to avoid using plastic stone in especially exposed positions such as copings, weatherings and cills. Its use even on quoins can be risky in some places.

A mixture of plastic and natural stone repairs carefully distributed over the same wall face will help to retain variety and colour in the finished result and counteract the tendency of plastic stone to develop a dreary uniformity. Few firms are prepared to undertake both methods, but satisfactory results have been obtained by two firms working simultaneously, one as subcontractor to the other.[7]

Precast stone

The surface of precast artificial stone simulates natural stone and is usually about 25 mm thick, covering a concrete core. Manufacturers have in recent years become very skilled in reproducing the texture of natural stone, particularly in rockfaced coursed rubble in the Bath stone area. Nevertheless, the advantage in price that precast holds over natural stone depends in part upon the use of standard dimensions and materials that can be produced in quantity. However acceptable such materials may be in new construction, this limits the suitability of precast stone for use in piecemeal repairs to existing buildings, whose details are characteristically variable. There are, however, at least three categories in which precast stone can play a useful role in the repair of existing masonry.

The first category is in the renewal of parapet and gable copings and roof ridges, where a constant section is normally maintained over long runs, and where there may be compelling reasons for not using natural stone. An appearance of dull uniformity during initial years can be avoided by ordering the sections to be delivered in two slightly varying tints (at small, if any, additional cost), but this has little permanent importance, since copings and ridges weather down so much more quickly than the rest of the building. A word of warning may be useful here. Coping joints are more likely to become defective between precast stones than between natural stones, because the concrete cores not only continue to shrink as the curing process completes itself but also remain liable to larger thermal and moisture movements than are found in natural stone. Adequate dowelling is important.[8]

Secondly, precast stone is useful for chimney caps, being likely to resist the strong acids in modern flue gases better than most natural stones. Durability can be increased by using high alumina cement in the preparation of the artificial stone surface, but it is wise to ask for preliminary tests on the compatibility of such cement with the stone aggregate that is to be used.

Thirdly, occasions can arise when precast stone will serve a useful purpose in the repair of window mullions. When the internal faces of the mullions are sound and it has already been decided for some good reason that the traceries of that window will be best repaired using plastic rather than natural stone, then precast rather than plastic stone is likely to prove a more suitable material for piecing in the external halves of individual stones in the mullions. Caution is however advised, and especial care will be needed to secure appropriate tooling.[9]

Tiles

At the beginning of this century, architect members of the Society for the Protection of Ancient Buildings introduced a method of repairing stone faces by removing decayed stone, cutting horizontal grooves into the sound stone behind and then rebuilding the face with tiles laid horizontally in mortar and bonded into the grooves. Sometimes the front edges of the tiles were left exposed and lime-washed over; elsewhere the tiled face was kept back and plastered over (although the plaster often failed with the passage of years). This is still an appropriate technique for local repairs on contracts where no masons are employed and it has often been used for refacing rectangular quoin stones. But cutting grooves and fitting tiles is a slow and extremely labour-intensive process, so that cost has become relatively high. Moreover, on many buildings the merits of the technique decrease as its use spreads. A few individual stones can be repaired in this way with advantage to the church as a whole, but widespread insertion of tiles will tend to destroy the textural unity of the building and may well complicate the problems that will confront repairers in later generations. A halt must be called before the whole elevation begins to acquire an ersatz flavour.

Bricks

Before condemning in principle the practice of repairing stone wall faces in brick, one should remember the delightful effect of mellow brick repairs on many churches carried out in the eighteenth century both to rubble facings and to stone quoins. Much depends upon colour, texture and scale.

chapter 9
Flint facing

Flintwork involves so many special problems that it deserves a section to itself. In Sussex there is little experience left of laying flints, and the highest skills are in short supply even at Brandon in Suffolk, which has been the largest centre for knapping since neolithic times. It is now often necessary for an architect to give the most elementary directions.

There are three main methods of building in flint: using uncut, knapped, or squared flints. Uncut flints (sometimes called cobbles) are built into the walls in their natural rounded shapes. Knapped flints (that is, flints that have been split across) are built into the wall to show the black split face bounded by the natural rounded perimeter. Squared flints are knapped but also have their sides split to reduce the area visible when built into a wall to a square or rectangular or other regular shape. Squared flints are difficult to obtain.

It is very difficult to build projecting angles in flintwork (which explains the frequent occurrence of circular flint towers in East Anglia). Square corners are built with brick or stone quoins and flush brick piers are frequently introduced at intervals along boundary walls. Squared flints are coursed with fine joints, but uncut and knapped flints are laid at random, or coursed, or even herring-boned; it is important that repairs should maintain harmony with old work around them. Owing to the very irregular shapes of the flints, joints tend to be very wide indeed in some places. To avoid shrinkage, such wide joints are often filled with flint chips. It may be useful to introduce horizontal bedjoints at about 900 mm intervals.

Constructionally, the principal difficulty lies in obtaining adequate bond between the flint face and the core of the wall behind. In repairing or rebuilding a wall face it is essential to build in occasional flints long enough to tail deeply into the core behind. Pieces of ashlar are often used for this purpose, following the example of William of Wykeham's work at Winchester. Recent experience seems to show that it is advisable to use a rather weaker mix for repointing large areas of flint facing than has been usual during the last 50 years. Wall cores behind are often so soft and sandy that a face formed with flints and mortar containing a large proportion of cement will have a very different factor of thermal expansion. Adhesion is however necessary, and reliable experience recommends mortar mixed in the proportion of one of cement, three of lime, and twelve of sand graded with very coarse grit to 6 mm. In some recent work pozzolanic mixes (as described on pages 26 and 33–6) have proved to be highly successful when used for bedding and repointing East Anglian flintwork. Much less water must be used than is usual with other materials because flints are almost entirely non-absorbent.[1]

It is quite common to discover that a large area of existing flint facing has detached itself from the core and is bulging progressively forward, so that if nothing is done it will fall off. After the face has been planked and strutted off the scaffold, it may be possible even in bad cases to save the original face by pointing open facing joints and then inserting at intervals dovetailed bonders in stone or concrete to act as anchors (spaced somewhat as wall-ties), after which cavities are progressively grouted solid.[2]

A further word can be added about the decorative flintwork panels that are so characteristic in East Anglia, in which stonework is shaped to represent traceried openings or monograms or inscriptions and then filled flush with tight-jointed squared flints. In the smaller openings the old craftsmen often did not rebate the stonework deeply enough, with the result that most of the too shallow flints have fallen out. It is good to remedy this where possible during repairs by recessing the stone backing more deeply. But the greatest problem arises when serious decay occurs in the stone surrounds and backs of such decorative flushwork. Complete renewal has often been necessary in order to save the feature, and many beautiful designs have been lost because this was thought to be too difficult or too expensive. Modern techniques again offer a new way of avoiding this dilemma. The stone can be conserved and, if desirable, built up again by a conservator using the methods described on pages 55 and 57 of Chapter 10. This has been done for the inscription below the east window of Blythburgh church. The original has been rescued and the cost was far lower than would have been that of replacement by a copy.[3]

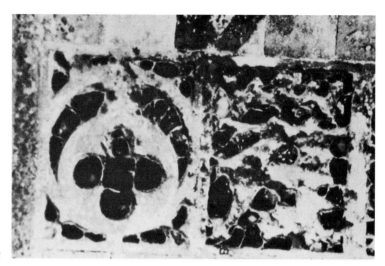

fig. 7a

fig. 7b
Treatment of
severely
decayed flint
flushwork
inscription by
poultice and
lime watering
with mortar
repairs and a
final shelter
coat: *a* before;
and *b* after.
Blythburgh,
Holy Trinity

© Peter Randall-Page

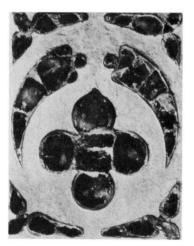

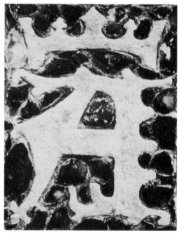

chapter 10
Conservators and conservation techniques

Hitherto we have been mainly discussing techniques that can be followed by builders and masons prepared to undertake the repair of old buildings, assisted in certain fields by commercial firms with specialist expertise. Until a very few years ago that was the only field from which architects could select the workforce needed for repair. Now there is a further option. Not only stone sculpture but also decaying architectural details can be conserved – to remain strengthened in approximately their present state if so desired. Professional conservators exist with practical experience of such work in the field (as distinct from experience in museums). They are also in touch with the latest scientific thinking. The number of men and women available with this competence is growing. One need today is that more architects should realise the existence of this option and should be prepared to explore it when suitable openings arise.[1]

So few conservators with skills in working on stone existed previously that their efforts were naturally concentrated almost exclusively on the preservation of irreplaceable masterpieces such as original figure sculpture. Now however it is possible to spread the net wider. Naturally such concentration of the highest technical skills can still only be applicable to very special cases – cost and the availability of suitable persons prohibit more – but there are many irreplaceable objects besides figure sculpture. Architectural details, such as the best foliage carving, must be included in this category and are even harder to move into a museum than statues. In work of such quality, where the slightest impression of the original sculptor's hand is valued, opposition to copying or restoration (or what is called pastiche) rises to its highest and the arguments in favour of preserving what remains, without attempt at imaginary reconstruction, are at their strongest. But every effort must be made to guard against the danger that this generation's methods of preservation do not create irremediable damage for all future generations.[2]

Worldwide interest in the possibility of consolidating and stabilizing stone in an active state of decay has been intense since the Second World War. Though the source of such interest has sprung mainly from the world of museums and national research institutes, progress is such that at least two processes are now available in Britain for application to the external stonework of buildings. Since at the time of writing we have less than 20 years' experience of either of the techniques, we suggest they should both be treated as experimental for the present. Neither process is yet suitable for application by the building industry; it would be wise at present to entrust such work to trained conservators or at least have it carried out under the direction of a consultant conservator.[3]

As the purpose of conservation is to preserve every fragment of the original, while at the same time preventing further decay, some degree of cleaning is, for reasons both technical and aesthetic, almost certain to be necessary before conservation can be attempted. In almost every case the cleaning method becomes an integral part of the conservation process and can itself have as great (if not greater) effect on the final appearance as the conservation process itself. This has not been understood in much of the controversy over the merits of alternative techniques.

Silane impregnation

The risks involved in the application of most chemical stone preservatives that have been suggested in the past have already been pointed out (see pages 9–10 and 29). They are unable to penetrate sufficiently deeply into the stone, with the result that any skin they create tends to get pushed off bodily by the build-up of salts behind the surface. But since the Second World War British scientists and conservators, after having experimented with many new chemicals, have mainly concentrated on a new type of consolidant made of chemicals called alkoxysilanes and known for short by the generic name of silanes. The basic principle is that the materials are prepared as 'monomers', which enables them to penetrate the stone much as would water, but that after some time-delay the molecules of the silane 'polymerize' in the stone and form three-dimensional lattice structures that set rigidly, holding the surrounding stonework firmly together and helping to immobilize harmful salts in the area penetrated. To the non-scientist this principle may seem miraculous but, once accepted, it sounds easy. Yet its application involves immense practical difficulties. In this country attempts at conservation using silanes were pioneered by the Victoria and Albert Museum and have been followed by the Building Research Establishment using a patented formula known as 'Brethane'. It is generally agreed that the result is not likely to prove lasting unless the rigidity imparted extends to a depth of more than 25 mm below the surface, deeper, that is, than the layer which is subject to the normal wetting–drying cycle. One major effort has therefore been to control the length of the time-delay before polymerization starts: if the delay is too short the silane will not have soaked in far enough and the exercise will be likely to induce harmful results similar to those associated with previous chemical preservatives. But if the delay is too long, some of the silane in its fluid monomer form may penetrate so far into the interior that the rest that is left in the outer 25 mm will not be strong enough to have any consolidating effects. The process seems in fact to be full of promise for the future, but must still be regarded as experimental.

Risks involved

It will be wise to reinforce this warning by mention of some of the risks involved.

There is a school of thought that demands that all conservation work should be 'reversible'. Others think that this has become a catchword: no worthwhile action on stonework taken by masons or any others is ever completely reversible. We are concerned with degrees of reversibility, which need to be assessed in every case. Yet it must be admitted that deep silane impregnation is completely irreversible; the treated material is no longer natural stone and can never be returned to its natural state. Secondly, it has been said to change the colour of the stone. But careful observation has shown that when applied correctly the colour change is so slight as to be negligible – far less in fact than the colour changes that rival methods of conservation cause. Thirdly, silaned stone will probably weather differently from natural stone, since moulds or lichens will no longer flourish upon it, though they have started to grow again on a treated stone head in St Paul's Churchyard and upon the Sandbach crosses. Fourthly, it will not take paint or limewash in the same way as natural stone. Lastly, it cannot be used by ordinary building labour. Summing up after some 14 years' experience of its use in the open, we know that some early examples of its use did not prove successful. Confidence in current judgement of the conditions under which the material can be used without risk of failure will increase as the span of years grows longer over which silaned repairs have continued to prove satisfactory. In the meantime, a decision to use silanes now should clearly be influenced by a judgement of whether the stones at issue are similar to many others or whether they have some special quality or interest or, indeed, whether they deserve to be considered uniquely irreplaceable so that no risks whatever would be justified. At the other extreme there can be strong arguments for the use of silanes to preserve the shape of an interesting artefact that is about to disintegrate and for which no other treatment is likely to be successful.

Cleaning

Stonework must be reasonably porous if silanes are to penetrate freely. An attempt to introduce silane through a blackened sulphated crust or into saturated stonework would be absurd and unlikely to succeed. Water cleaning cannot therefore be employed unless sufficient time is allowed to permit the stone to dry out thoroughly. The preferred method of cleaning is by air-abrasion, a very delicate process using pencil-sized instruments such as those distributed in England by G.E.C. Mechanical Handling Ltd, of Erith. A number of abrasives are available of which perhaps the most suitable are aluminium oxide or (if the stone has been covered by a layer of paint that must not be disturbed) glass 'beads' so fine that they look almost like talcum powder.

Vacuum impregnation

One way to assist silanes to penetrate deeply is to surround the stones to be treated with an air-and-liquid-tight envelope and then to create such a high vacuum that air is sucked out not only from the surface but even from the very core of the stone. The silane is then allowed to flow in, taking care to avoid air lock, and most of it disappears into the interior of the stone. This process is obviously better suited to the treatment of freestanding statues than to stones attached to a building, in which latter case the liquid is liable to flow through hidden internal fissures and reappear at the surface in unexpected places many metres away. This operation may involve so many risks that its use on valuable material should only be permitted under the most expert supervision. The Victoria and Albert Museum has achieved successful results. Messrs Balfour-Beatty hold a relevant patent.

Lime treatment

Reference has already been made to the treatment of limestones with lime water and their repair with lime mortar. The techniques have been further developed over the last 25 years by Professor Robert Baker and have been used extensively on such buildings as Iffley Parish Church, Croyland Abbey and the west fronts of Wells and Exeter Cathedrals.

Stone is first treated with a lime putty poultice applied hot from slaking and kept wet for between two to three weeks. On removal of the poultice much of the dirt and sulphated crusts will be found to have been softened and cleaning can be carried out by careful brushing assisted by water sprays. Air-abrasion equipment similar to that used in the silane process has been found useful in areas of particular delicacy.[4]

Cleaning all too often reveals previous repair carried out in entirely unsuitable material. These repairs must be removed and the stone then strengthened with up to 50 coats of clear lime water applied as a coarse drench and subsequently mopped off the stone to prevent surface crystallization.

Repairs are then carried out in pozzolanic lime mortars each specially formulated to match exactly the colour and texture of the surrounding stone. As lime water is hardly capable of consolidating very friable stone, such areas are normally scraped back and replaced in mortar textured to resemble the weathered surfaces found when conservation began. These mortar cappings are used to protect the weakest areas, but elsewhere the material is employed merely to fill cracks and crevices, many of which will be deliberately opened up to permit filling in depth. As the mortar is designed to be both weaker and more porous than the surrounding stone, its function is to act as a safety valve, providing a path through which the figure can dry out and to which the destructive salts will be

fig. 8a

fig. 8b
Thirteenth-
century foliage
spandrel: *a*
after cleaning;
b after repair
but before the
application of
a lime-based
shelter coat.
Wells
Cathedral

attracted should they continue to move after the treatment is complete. The mortar thus acts as a sacrificial addition to the stone rather than as a consolidant in its own right.

As cleaning opens the pores of the stone and thus makes it more vulnerable to acids deriving from the atmosphere, the final process is to apply a limewash slurry, bound with a small quantity of casein and coloured with ground stonedust. The slurry is applied wet and then rubbed into the surface. Such a shelter coat will afford some degree of protection but will not last for ever and renewal will in due course become necessary at least on the most exposed areas.[5]

Such a process is suitable only for limestone; it would be disastrous if applied to sandstones, and possibly even to magnesian limestones. Whereas silane treatments permit the conservator, once cleaning is finished, virtually to 'freeze' the form of the stone, a decision to use lime treatment implies a somewhat greater interference with the original material. Such interference may be unacceptable for ethical reasons and clearly should only be entrusted to an experienced conservator with great sensitivity to form. The treatment as here described would certainly be unacceptable for stonework intended for future viewing in museum-like conditions.

Recording

Architects should be aware of that basic discipline of the conservator that insists on the preparation of a full report on an object both before and after treatment, including an accurate account of materials and techniques used in the treatment. Estimates should not be sought from conservators without a stipulation that such records are to be prepared and subsequently lodged in safe keeping. The Council for the Care of Churches is the central repository for church conservation records and a second copy will frequently be required by the parish.

Conservators' records should attain as high a standard as their work, but architects need also to remember that they too have parallel (even if simpler) obligations, as has been pointed out in Chapter 6 (see page 23).

chapter 11
Conclusion

For some 200 years, and probably more, attempts have been made to find a cure for stone decay in buildings; almost without exception the 'cures' have proved useless or positively harmful. We hope as authors of this guide that we will not be considered over-gullible if we record our belief that over the past two decades real progress appears to have been made in developing new techniques, materials and skills.

What further developments are desirable and how can standards be raised further?

Despite one or two hopeful signs the British stone quarrying industry must be at a historically low ebb.[1] Rightly or wrongly masons report continued difficulty in obtaining regular supplies of reliable stone even from some of our most famous quarries, while yet more expensive foreign stones appear to be obtaining an increasing share of the market owing to the apparent inability of the British industry to compete. With the ever-increasing cost of labour it is essential (if we are to avoid waste) to use only the most trustworthy stones in the repair of historic structures. Yet there appears to be no quick, reliable and economic test that can be commissioned by the harassed architect to check on the lasting quality of new stone. An agreed technique for such testing is urgently required, both to vet the quality of stone from recently opened or unfamiliar quarries and to monitor the quality of the product from existing sources.

Architects who have read thus far will be well aware that, whatever the diversity of techniques that have been developed, it will not in practice be possible to specify them unless they are widely available through the building industry. The most sensitive care of historic structures is only likely to be achieved through the hands of multi-disciplinary craft teams; it is almost impossible to organize groups of specialist but independent subcontractors to work together amicably on contracts where a different technique may be necessary on every stone. We need fixer masons who can achieve excellent 'plastic' repairs in mortar and also be responsible for cleaning, and cleaners who can turn their hand to both water washing and air-abrasion as may be best for the individual stone in question.

Masons and, in particular, conservation architects have much to learn from the conservators on the degree to which external stonework can be consolidated and repaired rather than destroyed and renewed. It is at present uncertain where the balance will eventually settle between these alternative policies. What is clear is that the traditional skills of the mason as stone cutter and fixer will always be required and that those techniques necessary for the care, cleaning and preservation of plain and moulded stonework should remain with the masons' trade. Only where it is possible to save original carved detail need consideration be given to consulting the conservator. It is already encouraging to note two or three firms of masons who have recently forged close links with conservators or offered them employment.

The organization of the care of historic buildings in this country is fragmented – at least if compared with the continent of Europe – and the scale of the typical contract is rightly small. It is essential if standards are to be maintained (let alone raised) that the technical advisory services provided by central government, one of the amenity societies, and the Church of England should continue and be strengthened. It is equally important that amenity and learned societies, along with the Council for the Care of Churches and Diocesan Advisory Committees, should continue to promote debate on techniques and standards and organize gatherings where trades, professions and advisers can meet and discuss.

Finally, we must reiterate that development of our present expertise is totally dependent on a sufficient flow of money to ensure that skilled craftsmen are given continuity of employment. The relatively recent extension of central government grants to ecclesiastical buildings in use may prove in practice to have the most long-term effect of all developments referred to in this paper.

Notes

chapter 1

1   It is pleasant to record a significant resurgence in the British quarrying industry. Refer to *The Natural Stone Directory*, Herald House Ltd compiled annually by Natural Stone Specialist (monthly).

2   Levels of sulphur emissions have decreased dramatically in recent years (though the chemical effects of past emissions still lie within existing stonework); levels of nitrous oxides continue to increase.

3   The introduction of state aid to churches and cathedrals has had a fundamental effect in retaining and developing craft skills.

chapter 2

1   This view should be contrasted with applications aiming either to dry out the wall core or reduce *internal* decay. It would be fair to record that the statement reflects British practice and would be questioned by many Italian conservators, for whom attempts to make the external surface hydrophobic have in some areas been the norm.

2   The Care of Churches Ecclesiastical Jurisdiction Measure 1991 abolished Archdeacons' certificates. Archdeacons can now grant faculties for certain uncontroversial matters (Section 14).

chapter 3

1   Technology, in the form of a range of non-destructive inspection systems, can now extend the ability of the architect in assessing durability and the maintenance needs of masonry and building fabric: using these systems takes some of the guesswork out of planning, and often circumvents both costly surprises during the course of a repair programme and unwanted return to repairs after only a few years.

The main techniques of radar, thermography, acoustic and magnetic testing can produce valuable data when appropriately applied. For example, years of unexplained damp penetration may be explained, or the extent of de-lamination of a flint facing from a rubble wall can be revealed: similarly, unequivocal evidence of the structural form and integrity of a wall may be established in a few minutes, without any damage or invasion of the fabric.

PCCs or owners should not be dazzled by the technology however, as it is only as good as the people using it and the expertise they bring; providers of these techniques must bring an understanding of and sympathy for the architectural and structural issues. Costs are significant, because the equipment is expensive, but the value of these techniques lies in the factual base that is brought to the process of planning, specification and programming.

For further reading see *Non-destructive Investigation and recording of standing structures* by GBG Ltd with Historic Scotland, published by Technical Advice Historic Scotland, TAN 2000, or contact George Ballard, GBG Ltd, Swaffham Bulbeck, Cambridge.

2 Since 1984 the development of hydraulic hoists has greatly reduced the cost of making preliminary investigations. Equipment can be hired with an operative; on occasion a suitably trained surveyor can act as 'driver'. Electrically powered vehicles are available for internal inspections that can pass through a large-sized domestic door and still reach 18–20 metres. (a) The introduction of the Construction Design Management (CDM) Regulations in 1996 means that all such questions, including those involving future maintenance, should be tackled before work is begun. For all works of any scope the building owner or PCC is required under the law to appoint a suitably qualified and competent Planning Supervisor and Principal Contractor, who must in turn plan, co-ordinate and document matters of health and safety.

chapter 4

1 The general principles set out in the section on cleaning remain sound but much has changed in the technical detail. Claims have been made that full petrological investigations should be carried out by an independent consultant before any cleaning is carried out of historic stonework. In the light of damage caused to a number of vulnerable stones, particularly including argillaceous Scottish sandstone, such claims can be justified, but to apply them to all stone – particularly the easily cleaned limestones – would impose entirely unnecessary costs, for such investigations are not cheap. The challenge to the architect is to decide when such prior investigation is essential and to whom to entrust the work. Current practitioners should note:

a) The BS has been amended three times since the original publication. BS 6270 parts 1 &2 are now superseded by BS 8221 parts 1 &2 2000. BS 6270 Part 3 1991 (cleaning of metals) is still current.

b) Pressure washing of sound limestones can be most effective and make remarkable reductions in the use of water – itself a very dangerous 'chemical' when stone is impregnated with salt. Experiments should be made with different pressures and nozzles, 2000 psi seems remarkably high. Cambridgeshire clunch cleaned most effectively at 600 psi so 2000 psi is probably inappropriately high. One advantage of the technique, which should of course never be used on delicate stone bearing traces of mediaeval detail, is that it knocks away loose scabs and pointing. (See also Repointing, page 25.) The relatively recent technique of sponge blasting involves bombarding the stone with minute particles of sponge, which are less abrasive than grains of sand and do not involve the use of water.

c) The invention of new patented cleaning methodologies, particularly JOS and DOFF by Stonehealth Ltd (Marlborough), has transformed the process of stone cleaning into a much more precise and delicate art in the hands of experience practitioners. JOS involves the application of water and air with mild abrasives through special nozzles which lift dirt at much lower pressures. DOFF uses water at high temperature and controlled pressure. JOS and DOFF can only be used by licensed companies; nevertheless care in application is still required, and fine detail must often be cleaned by other methods.

d) Increasing concern has developed over the use of chemicals to clean whole buildings, perhaps in contrast to their limited use by experts on sculpture and memorials. There have been too many instances of unfortunate subsequent developments, usually due to failure to remove the material from the stone. Much damage has been caused in the past by use of caustic soda on limestone, actively promoting decay by salts though it remains a reasonably safe way of removing dried-out oil paint, perhaps after application by poultice. Risk can be reduced by subsequent dry removal, for washing-off can drive the material deeper into the stone.

e) Water should never be used on alabaster now that the alternative techniques are available. It is doubtful that disking should ever be used.

f) Though some lichens can cause damage – and most mosses will do so as they hold water on the face of the stone – many lichens appear to have no ill effects. The partial removal of lichen by dry brushing, carried out in 1997 on the West Front of Salisbury Cathedral, is an example to be evaluated.

g) Readers will be aware of the many technical advances made since the first edition in the development of small, medium and large-scale equipment for cleaning masonry, particularly the production of more sensitive tools for the application of air abrasive.

h) The use of the word 'poultice' can be confusing. A poultice can be used to keep an active chemical – even one such as water – against the face of the surface under treatment for a 'dwell-time', determined after test. Alternatively, a poultice may be applied to a saturated surface and allowed to dry, this in an attempt to remove salts from the stone. These are two very different operations. The problem with poulticing is that the surface being worked on is concealed and so unexpected developments cannot be monitored.

i) The desirability of initial trials and combining methods so as to reduce risk and also, if necessary, re-testing during and after the works, cannot be emphasized too strongly. To state that 'if damage occurs, STOP and consult' should be the basis of more specifications.

chapter 5

1 Where internal surfaces have been significantly contaminated by salts, whether deposited by rising damp, by bird droppings or by careless storage on the wall outside, loss of surface can in some instances be delayed by controlling the internal environment so as to avoid the level of relative humidity at which the particular salts go into and out of solution. But see Price, C A and Brimblecombe, P, 'Preventing salt damage in porous materials' in *Preventive Conservation: Practice, Theory and Research,* London Institute for Conservation, 1994, pp. 90-93 on the complexities that arise where a number of salts are present.

2 Significant advances have been made in the last 15 years in the knowledge of how to use lime mortar, though there is yet more to learn. Where buildings are constructed in lime there should be a presumption *against* the use of any cement-based products except where specifically justified.

chapter 6

1 The greater availability of hydraulic hoists has, to a limited extent, altered the balance since 1984. Inspections, and even some light maintenance, can now be carried out from such equipment more cheaply than when scaffold had to be erected.

2 The role of the mason in preliminary decision-making is more difficult to arrange now that work has subsequently to be put to competitive tender in many cases. Nevertheless, where significant technical problems exist (for example, in the treatment of argillaceous sandstones) or where additional advice is required, there are now, as compared with 1984, a number of consultants capable of offering independent professional advice, carrying out tests and preparing analyses.

3   The need to prepare adequate records of the condition of historic structures before works are put in hand is of ever-increasing importance. Such records not only form the basis of contractual documentation but are also a pre-requirement for any archaeological/analytical examination of the historic structure. They are also essential for the final recording of what actually has been carried out. The preparation of such record drawings, however prepared, is frequently required by grant-makers and may itself be eligible for grant-aid. Photogrammetric survey drawings have come into their own with the advent of computers and computer drawing. A survey can now be supplied for immediate use on CAD software, ready for repairs to be marked on. The stone-by-stone detail given on these drawings is invaluable in enabling an accurate marking up of repairs, quantification for cost purposes and (given the computer facility) swift amendment for progress and final as-built drawings. The additional cost of photogrammetry over rectified photography is often outweighed by the advantages listed above, which must also include savings in architects'/surveyors' time. English Heritage publishes guidance notes on surveying methods including photogrammetry and standard formats for computer drawings.

4   Nobody could object to the dating of new stonework or even the commemoration of a firm or individual, if carried out with discretion (the parallel would be 'plumbers' marks'). However, it is the properly deposited drawing that should be the final record.

chapter 7

1   There is a particular risk of damage by angle-grinders, if carelessly used. However, with effective training and supervision, they can be the most effective and risk-free method of removing hard cement from soft stonework.

2   In the intervening years since this book was originally published, there have been considerable developments in the use of suitable mortars for pointing stonework. It is now possible for the contractor to purchase lime putty from large manufacturers, such as Tilcon, and a considerable number of small companies have grown up to supply the putty together with suitable sands mixed as 'coarse stuff'. Additionally, the use and availability of hydraulic lime has substantially increased over the past ten years.

Whereas, in certain circumstances, there is still benefit to be gained by using a cement based mortar, the extent of such circumstances has been considerably reduced. Experience has shown that lime-based mortars using both lime putty and hydraulic lime can withstand the vagaries of the British climate. There appears to be a general consensus that the use of lime-based mortar for pointing without the introduction of cement should be considered the norm and that the use of cement is largely restricted to particularly exposed areas or where sandstone is used.

Where a lime mortar is used with lime putty as the major constituent, the use of a setting agent is still necessary to achieve a pozzolanic effect. (Whilst the science is still developing, at present Polstar 501 is the ingredient most often recommended.) As for lime putty, the availability of Polstar and other similar setting materials has increased and these are now to be supplied by a number of specialist firms throughout the country.

Research shows that the use of cement in mortars of 1:3:12 (cement: lime: sand) or weaker should be avoided, as it is detrimental to the strength of the mix.

In those situations where hydraulic lime is used, it is essential that the lime does not contain any cement. In the past, particularly with European hydraulic limes, it has been difficult to ascertain whether such cement is present within the pre-mixed packages. However, this is becoming less problematic. Nonetheless, care should be taken to ensure that the constituents of the hydraulic lime are known before they are used.

Bibliographical Note:

The use of *The Building Conservation Directory,* published annually by Cathedral Communications Ltd, is particularly beneficial in identifying firms who will provide Polstar, lime putty, coarse stuff etc.

A summary of the Smeaton Report papers will be published in 2001 in the English Heritage Research Transactions, published by James & James. See also:

Ashurst & Ashurst: *Mortars, Plasters and Renders* English Heritage Practical Building Conservation Guide, Vol 3, Gower Technical Press, 1988

J.M. Teutonico (ed.): *The English Heritage Directory of Building Limes,* Donhead, 1997

3   One of the best methods of reducing suction and preparing joints after cutting out sound stonework for repointing is to wash down the wall with a medium-pressure water lance, thus introducing water and washing away dust and loose materials.

4   The use of austenitic (316 marine grade) stainless steel is now of course normal practice.

5   With hindsight, the suggestion of setting prepared iron in cement washes or even in epoxy would appear unwise. Where the rusting of saddle-bars is causing stone to break up, it would now be normal to remove the ferramenta and tip the ends in either stainless steel or bronze before resetting. Where such treatment is too expensive, careful opening up around the tips, treatment of the exposed surfaces with a rust inhibitor and subsequent repointing, perhaps with the introduction of a mastic or other soft material which can accept further expansion, is a cheaper alternative. In all cases, it is wise to cut off the bottoms of stanchions where buried in cills and to point up the mortice.

6   Judicious introduction of leadwork can reduce costs as well as the unnecessary destruction/replace-ment of original stone. If loss of the lip of a weathering has exposed the head of stone below, the weathering action can be restored in lead without the need for stone renewal. Equally, the eroded and water-holding surface of a stringcourse can be retained if built up in weak mortar and weathered in lead. Where exposed to high winds, the front edge can be welted over a continuous stainless steel strip and secured into the stone parpends.

7   The warning should be repeated against using hydrophobic chemicals in an attempt to consolidate external weakened and exfoliating surfaces, *see* note 1 under Chapter 2.

8   Subsequent experience of lime treatments over the last 30 years has given further grounds for confidence in its effectiveness, despite evidence that most of the lime is deposited in only the outer few millimetres of the stone. Regular inspection of the figure sculpture at Wells Cathedral, for example, has shown that the treated figures have remained in much better condition than might have been expected. The success of the technique is now commonly attributed to the protective action of the shelter coat and to the skilful use of lime mortars to fill cracks and to prevent the ingress of water. The hot lime poultice is now seldom used, having been replaced by other cleaning techniques and because it is not possible to monitor the effect of the poultice on the face of the stone.

A further development of the technique lies in the application of protective shelter coats (see below) to large areas of masonry that have not received any prior treatment with lime, other than mortar repairs. The West Front of Rochester Cathedral, cleaned under the direction of Martin Caroe in 1991, is a notable example.

9   Practice has moved on, as anticipated in the original text. The term 'plastic' stone is now rarely used, and well-trained masons are capable of carrying out good quality mortar repairs in either pozzolanic or cement-based mortars. Perhaps the best work is being carried out when stone conservators are integrated with the masonry team under suitable contractual conditions.

10   It would appear that the authors were referring to ill-experienced contractors. All competent masons can point to standards equal to those of the average conservator.

11   Most would now agree that repairs in mortar should be confined to dentistry techniques, and only in the most exceptional circumstances should mortar be used to replace a complete stone. Though in expert hands it is usually possible to arrive at mixes that not only match their surroundings but also weather in a similar manner, such standards are not easily reached. The task is made easier if the area of the repair is kept just *behind* the adjacent face and then textured to resemble decayed stone, the resulting contrast reducing any effect of differential weathering. Whereas feather-edging is generally to be discouraged in repairs to the masonry, it was frequently resorted to by conservators working on the west front of Wells Cathedral, and subsequent inspections have shown no ill effects.

12   The quality of the brickdust as a pozzolanic additive is important. English Heritage have, since the late 1980s, been conducting research on the use and strength of lime mortars, and particularly the practice of 'gauging' lime with cement. The research found that any use of cement in mortars weaker than 1:3:12 is detrimental to the strength of the mix. A summary of the Smeaton Report papers will be published in 2001 in the English Heritage Research Transactions, published by James & James.

13   Every project poses a different challenge in harmonizing the new work with the old, but the following can be helpful in achieving a general harmony:

(a)   Deciding on the area to be treated. The selection of a distinct architectural entity – an aisle, a bay, a window or a buttress – improves the likelihood of success.

(b)   Deciding on the degree of pre-cleaning that is technically possible and affordable. In many cases the introduction of clean new stone and pointing into a cleaned old wall is the ideal.

(c)   The tooling of new stonework. Develop a sympathetic tooling of new surfaces so that textures between new and weathered are in harmony. Never artificially 'distress', but avoid new stonework looking like processed cheese.

(d)   Make use of the recessed mortar repair technique.

(e)   On occasion use mortar repairs to clarify the 'design' of eroded features, for example to emphasize an arris or to disguise the projecting flat bed of a new mullion beneath old tracery. It is surprising what the eye can appreciate with the addition of such minor hints.

(f)   Use limited shelter coats to protect both new and old stone and to reduce contrasts in colour. Eventually such shelter coats will largely weather away, by which time the stones themselves will have weathered in.

Notes

1   Unfortunately the Geological Museum no longer provides free advice on stone selection. There are a number of consultants in this field who will analyse existing stonework and advise on possible replacements that are currently being worked. There is also *The Natural Stone Directory.*

2   All quarried stone, but particularly Clunch and other softer stones, should be allowed to mature for at least four seasons prior to use in repairs. The stone dries, hardens and defects can be revealed after exposure to a frost. Sandstones can swell marginally when released from the ground pressure. These transformations need to be allowed time to occur before stone is used in repairs.

3   Now that computer-controlled saws are widely available, there is little likelihood of masons being unwilling to use any suitable machine aids, nor risk that the traditional craft skills will disappear.

4   Preservation of original joint lines should be the norm, with changes made only in exceptional circumstances, for example to preserve original detail. Specifiers should be aware that in general it costs little more to piece in a medium-sized stone than a small 'mason'. Particular care should be taken to avoid piecing small 'masons' into regularly jointed formal ashlar owing to the resulting changes in rhythm and scale. Such work is frequently necessary when repairing eighteenth-century masonry put together with iron cramps. Hence the recessed mortar repair can be a useful device, reducing costs, preserving original mortar and avoiding alterations in scale. (See note 11 under Chapter 7).

5   Comments on the 'drabness' of plastic repair arise from work carried out in mixes based on ordinary Portland cement (OPC). Mixes based on white OPC do not suffer in the same way. Nevertheless, it is best to avoid the use of cement wherever possible and confine plastic (mortar) repairs to dentistry, with the possible exception of the repair of voussoirs, where much expense and destruction can be avoided by the use of the technique.

6   The repairs to Pulborough were carried out during a period when dimensioned Sussex sandstone was utterly unobtainable. They were brilliantly executed by 'Old Scarfe', a mason of vast experience, and stand well.

7   As previously stated, the majority of good masons are capable of carrying out both natural and mortar repairs to stonework. It is worth reiterating the advice that, in general, mortar repairs should be confined to dentistry and rarely, if ever, used on water-shedding surfaces.

8   Copings are best renewed in natural stone unless cost savings are essential. Specifiers should be aware of the thermal/moisture movement in concrete and how much more difficult it is to avoid open parpends in concrete copings as compared to stone.

9   Natural stone should clearly be the first choice. Whatever initial appearances, experience has shown that precast stone will never weather in harmony with natural stonework.

chapter 9

1   It has been found generally unwise to repoint flint facing to masonry constructed in lime with a mortar stronger than the core, particularly when it is so difficult to achieve a bond between facing and core. Rather, the solution should be to 'bring forward' the original bedding mortar. Recent work in this manner on the west tower of Ufford St Mary is standing well.

2   Use of stainless steel pins, always angled downward, should be considered, after which any gaps can be grouped with highly penetrative sulphur-free pozzolanic grout, similar to the 'St Paul's grout' developed for that cathedral.

3   Not only were costs lower but the destruction of original material was also totally avoided. The problem of how to treat the severely decayed, but blank, central stone was overcome by reversing the piece.

chapter 10

1   As readers will be aware, the current availability of specialist skills and professional advice would have amazed the original authors.

2   All cases must be decided on their merits. Objections are likely to be voiced against the destruction and falsifications involved in attempts to add twentieth-century features to ancient sculpture. There is likely to be less objection to the removal of ancient work at risk and its replacement with an excellent copy, provided the removal can be carried out safely. Skills in the development of accurate 'copy-carving' are at last developing. However, the removal of precious stonework indoors can be risky as the resulting drying-out can lead to further loss of surface and, in the worst cases, to attack by soluble salts.

3   The number of consolidants available for use on external stone has continued to grow: it would be fair to say that in the UK, as opposed to certain continental European countries, there remains considerable caution over their use on historic stonework. Certainly, it is clear that none is a 'once and for all' panacea, and possibly only those that are proved by tests to be re-treatable as their effect reduces should be specified. Information is hard to come by, particularly from the trade. Brethane was applied to the heavily decayed voussoirs of the West Tower of York Minster in the early 1980s as the only possible way of preserving the stonework. By the mid 1990s it was agreed to have failed and the voussoirs were replaced by Rory Young.

4   Few, if any, conservators now use the classic hot-lime poultice, which is time-consuming and expensive and would appear to have no effect in strengthening the stone. Other safer cleaning techniques are available.

5   In present practice the significance of shelter coating is somewhat greater than implied by the short note above. The technique is applied more often than not at the conclusion of cleaning and repair works, both for its protective properties and also to aesthetically harmonize the completed repair programme.

   ● Shelter coating should always be carried out by experienced craftspeople and carefully monitored. The temptation to see the technique as a cure-all, or to conceal deficiencies or haste in repairs or pointing should be strenuously avoided.

   ● The technique is normally used in small areas, or on specific friable stones.

   ● Wholesale application, as on the West Front of Rochester Cathedral, or on the Central Tower at Wells Cathedral is rare, and in these instances was only undertaken to harmonize façades that had been substantially cleaned – to 'bring forward' areas that looked less clean and to help the whole weather down naturally together.

- A lime-rich shelter coat will give some of the benefits of lime water, will fill pores and micro-cracks which would otherwise trap water and help delay the build-up of harmful pollutant deposits on areas which are not washed by the weather.

- The shelter coat is a sacrificial coating and will erode away over a period of time, dependent on exposure. It should be thinly applied and is often 'bagged' or rubbed off after application to allow the character of the natural stone to grin through.

- The shelter coat should not conceal detail; application should not be made over traces of polychrome without good reason.

- Specifications should always require a minimum of three sample areas (at least I m²) of the coating to check that texture and colour match the existing as closely as possible.

chapter 11

1   As was observed in note 1 to the Introduction, there has been a significant resurgence in the quarrying industry in Britain.

Bibliography

Arnold, L 'The preservation of stone by impregnation with silanes', in Council for Places of Worship (now Council for the Care of Churches) *Newsletter*, no. 24, 1978

Ashurst, John *Cleaning Stone and Brick* (Technical Pamphlets, 4), Society for the Protection of Ancient Buildings, 1977

Ashurst, John *Mortars, Plasters and Renders in Conservation*, Ecclesiastical Architects' and Surveyors' Association, 1983

Ashurst, John and *Stone in Building: its Use and Potential Today*, Dimes, Francis G. Architectural Press, 1977

British Standards *British Standard Code of Practice for Cleaning and* Institution *Surface Repair of Buildings. Part I: Natural Stone, Cast Stone and Clay and Calcium Silicate Brick Masonry.* BS 6270: Part I, 1982

Building Research Digests No. 113, *Cleaning External Surfaces of Buildings* Establishment No. 125, *Colourless Treatments for Masonry* No. 139, *Control of Lichens, Moulds and Similar Growths* No. 177, *Decay and Conservation of Stone Masonry*

Caroe, Alban D.R. *Old Churches and Modern Craftsmanship*, Oxford University Press, 1949

Clarke, B.L. *Stone Preservation Experiments*, Building Research and Ashurst, John Establishment, 1972

Cooper, M. I. *Laser Cleaning in Conservation*, Butterworth-Heinemann, 1998

Council for the *Conference on New Materials in the Conservation of* Care of Churches *Churches*, 24 November 1981: transcript of papers and discussions, CCC, 1981

Davey, Norman *Building Stones of England and Wales*, Bedford Square Press, for the Standing Conference for Local History, 1976

Davey, Norman   *A History of Building Materials*, Phoenix House, 1961

Honeyborne, David B.   'Harmful interactions between building materials' in *SPAB News*, vol. 2, nos 3 and 4, July and October, 1981

Honeyborne, David B. and Price, Clifford A.   'Decay mechanisms in porous limestones', in *SPAB News*, vol. 1, nos 1 and 2, January/February and April 1980

Krubeis, W. et al.   'Microbial interaction with building stones with special reference to various cleaning and restoration techniques', in *Stone Cleaning*, 1993, pp. 237–8

Larson, John   'The conservation of stone monuments in churches', in (eds) John Ashurst and Francis G. Dimes, *Conservation of Buildings and Decorative Stone*, vol. 2, Butterworth-Heinemann, 1990

Larson, John   *Sculpture Conservation: Treatment or Reintegration?* Philip Lindley (ed.), Scholar Press, 1997

Plowden, Anna and Halaham, Frances   *Looking after Antiques*, Pan, 1997

Powys, A. R.   *Repair of Ancient Buildings*, 1929; Society for the Protection of Ancient Buildings, 1981 (reprint)

Price, Clifford A.   *The Decay and Preservation of Natural Building Stone*, Building Research Establishment, 1975

Proudfoot, T. and Rowell, C.   'The display and conservation of sculpture at Petworth', in *Sculpture Conservation*, Scholar Press, 1997

Schaffer, R.J.   *The Weathering of Natural Building Stones*, 1932; Building Research Establishment, 1972 (reprint with new Appendix)

Smith, John F.   *A Critical Bibliography of Building Conservation: Historic Towns, Buildings, their Furnishings and Fittings*, Mansell, 1978

Wilimzig, M., Sand, W. and Bock, E.   'The importance of stone cleaning on micro-organisms and microbial influence on corrosion', in *Stone Cleaning*, 1993, pp. 235–6

Index